GW01564395

STEPPING STONES 3

ACTIVITY BOOK

Julie Ashworth ■ John Clark

Name:	....
Class:	....
Teacher:	....
School:	....
Age:	....
Nationality:	....
Address:	....
Telephone number:	....

Nelson

Opposites

What's the opposite of big?   Small.

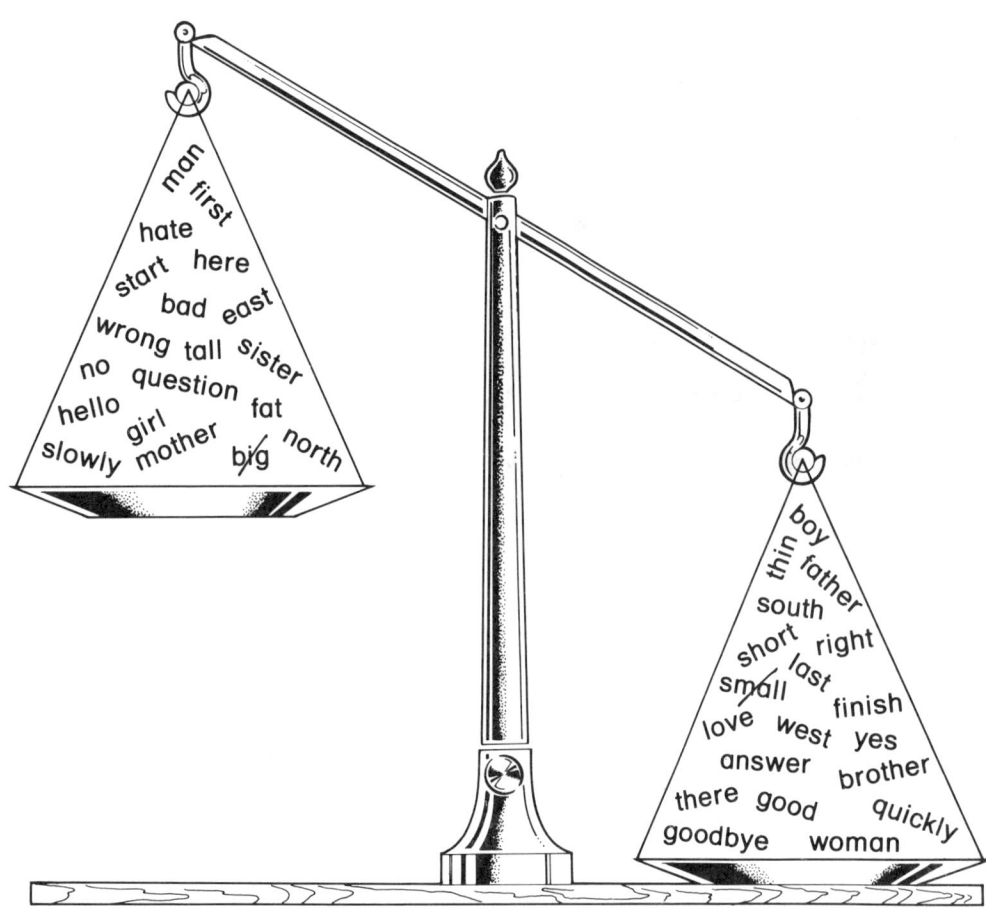

big	small

Write the opposite of these words in the crossword.

Across	Down
2 last	**1** small
4 west	**3** finish
5 wrong	**6** boy
8 mother	**7** answer
10 hate	**8** thin
11 brother	**9** short
12 yes	

Kong Mouse is a fat, greedy mouse. He's always eating. He loves cheese and biscuits. He also likes ice-cream, cake, chocolate, apples and oranges. The only things Kong doesn't like are vegetables. His sister, Tong, is just the opposite. She eats very little. She never eats fruit, cake, chocolate or ice-cream, but she does like cheese and biscuits. She also likes carrots, potatoes and beans.

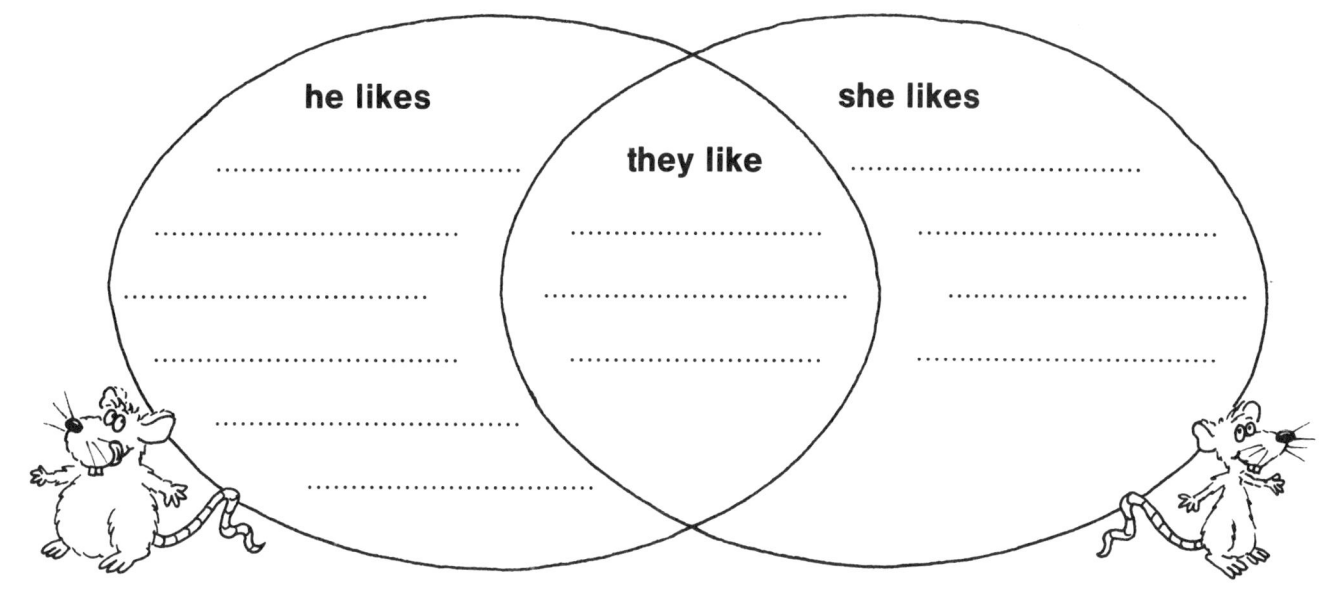

he likes

they like

she likes

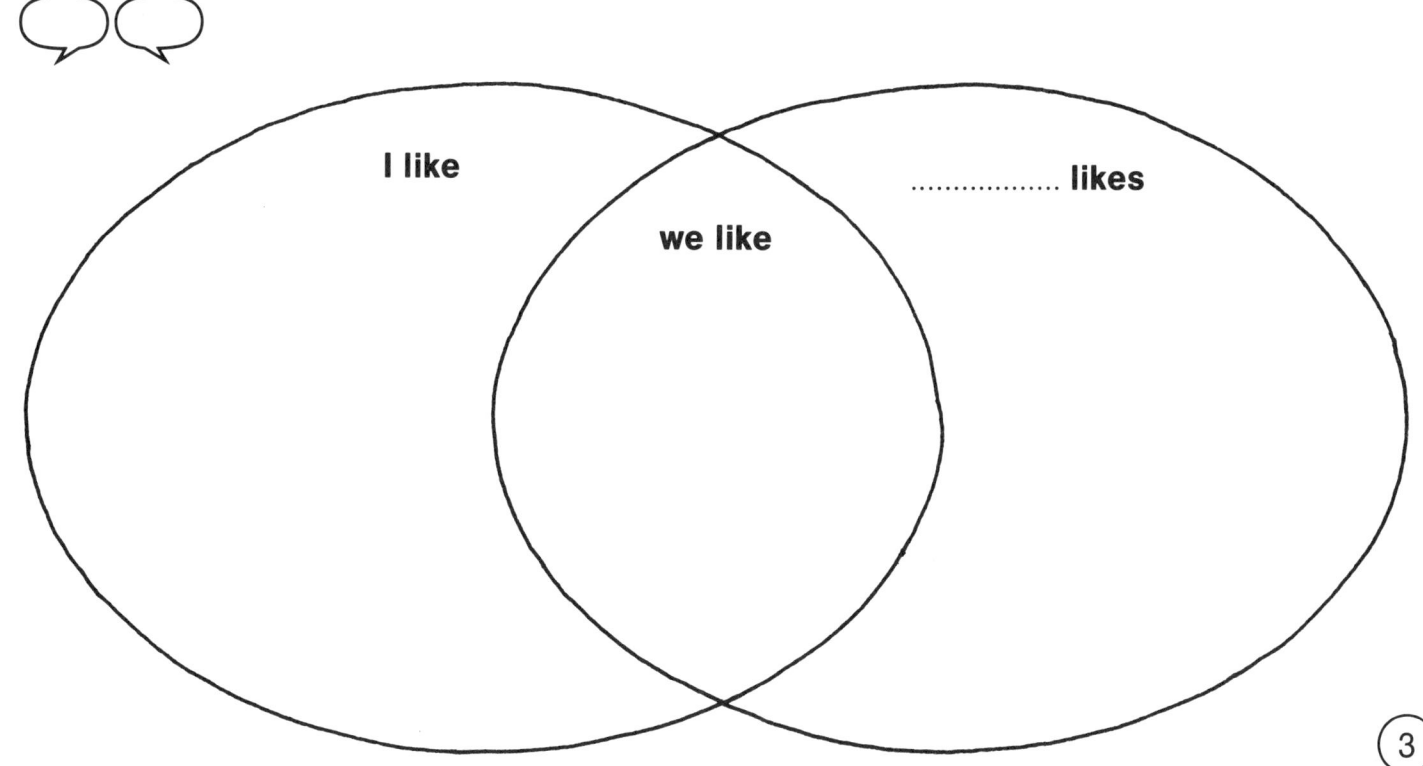

I like

we like

.... **likes**

	Write the names here.
Find someone who is tall.	
Find someone who is short.	
Find someone who has got long hair.	
Find someone who has got short hair.	
Find someone who can swim.	
Find someone who can't swim.	
Find someone who likes ice-cream.	
Find someone who doesn't like ice-cream.	

1 ....

2 ....

1 ....

2 ....

1 ....

2 ....

Take the third letter in   ....

The second letter in    ....

The second letter in    ....

The fourth letter in    ....

The last letter in    ....

The sixth letter in    ....

And the first letter in   ....

What have you got?

Draw your answer.

Opposites

John is the smallest. Dave is taller than John but shorter than Ben. Ben is taller than Jim but Jim is taller than Dave.

....

Mary is taller than Ann and Jane. Jane has got longer hair than Ann but Tina has got longer hair than Jane. Ann is taller than Tina and she's got the shortest hair.

....

	Name	Age	Birthday
1			
2			
3			
4			
5			
6			

Ask your friends: When's your birthday? How old are you?

CALENDAR

January						
1	2	3	4	5	6	7
8	9	10	11	12	13	
14	15	16	17	18	19	
20	21	22	23	24	25	
26	27	28	29	30	31	

July						
1	2	3	4	5	6	7
8	9	10	11	12	13	
14	15	16	17	18	19	
20	21	22	23	24	25	
26	27	28	29	30	31	

February						
1	2	3	4	5	6	7
8	9	10	11	12	13	
14	15	16	17	18	19	
20	21	22	23	24	25	
26	27	28	(29)			

August						
1	2	3	4	5	6	7
8	9	10	11	12	13	
14	15	16	17	18	19	
20	21	22	23	24	25	
26	27	28	29	30	31	

March						
1	2	3	4	5	6	7
8	9	10	11	12	13	
14	15	16	17	18	19	
20	21	22	23	24	25	
26	27	28	29	30	31	

September						
1	2	3	4	5	6	7
8	9	10	11	12	13	
14	15	16	17	18	19	
20	21	22	23	24	25	
26	27	28	29	30		

April						
1	2	3	4	5	6	7
8	9	10	11	12	13	
14	15	16	17	18	19	
20	21	22	23	24	25	
26	27	28	29	30		

October						
1	2	3	4	5	6	7
8	9	10	11	12	13	
14	15	16	17	18	19	
20	21	22	23	24	25	
26	27	28	29	30	31	

May						
1	2	3	4	5	6	7
8	9	10	11	12	13	
14	15	16	17	18	19	
20	21	22	23	24	25	
26	27	28	29	30	31	

November						
1	2	3	4	5	6	7
8	9	10	11	12	13	
14	15	16	17	18	19	
20	21	22	23	24	25	
26	27	28	29	30		

June						
1	2	3	4	5	6	7
8	9	10	11	12	13	
14	15	16	17	18	19	
20	21	22	23	24	25	
26	27	28	29	30		

December						
1	2	3	4	5	6	7
8	9	10	11	12	13	
14	15	16	17	18	19	
20	21	22	23	24	25	
26	27	28	29	30	31	

I am .... tall.

I am taller than ....

I am shorter than ....

I've got longer hair than ....

I'm younger than ....

I'm older than ....

Write more sentences in your exercise book.

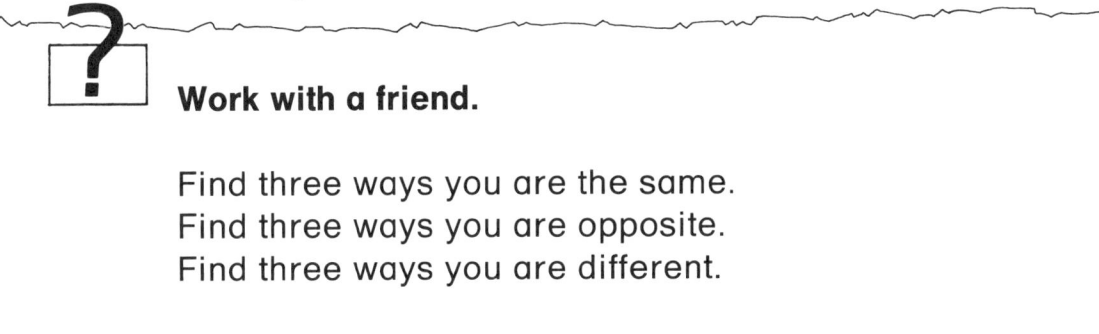

? Work with a friend.

Find three ways you are the same.
Find three ways you are opposite.
Find three ways you are different.

Put the lines in order. Look and guess.
Which line is the longest? Which line
is the shortest?

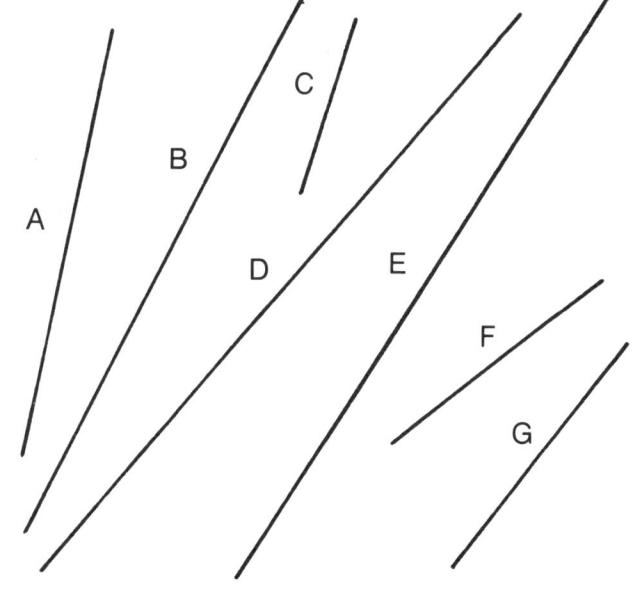

....

Now measure the lines with a ruler.
Were you right?

Which of these matches is the longest?
Look and guess.

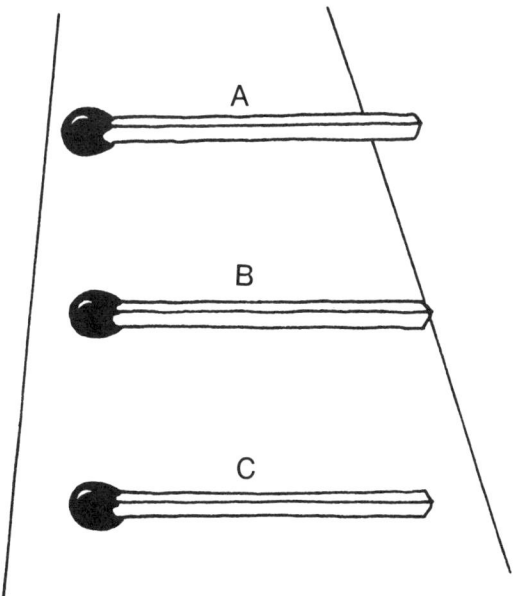

Match .... is the longest.
Measure them with a ruler. Were you
right?

Opposites

This ghost is in the picture on page 6 of your Coursebook.
Draw the ghost in the box. Which ghost is it?
Which room is it in?

	B2	D3	A2	E4	F3	C2
	H2	C4	G4	E5	F5	H1
	A4	E2	B3	G1	D2	G3
	G2	F4	B4	G5	E3	H3
	D4	H4	C3	A3	F1	F2

	1	2	3	4	5
A					
B					
C					
D					
E					
F					
G					
H					

Answer Bob's questions.

1 ? name your What's
   = *What's your name?*
   ....

2 ? live you do Where
   =
   ....

3 ? TV watching like you Do
   =
   ....

4 ? pet a got you Have
   =
   ....

5 ? piano the play you Can
   =
   ....

Mirror Images

ABCDEFGHIJKLMN OPQRSTUVWXYZ

1 Look at the letters in the mirror.

The letter **A** is upside down.
The letter **B** looks the same.

What happens to the other letters of the alphabet?
Which letters do you think look the same?

....

Now look in a mirror. Were you right?

2 Look at the letters in the mirror.

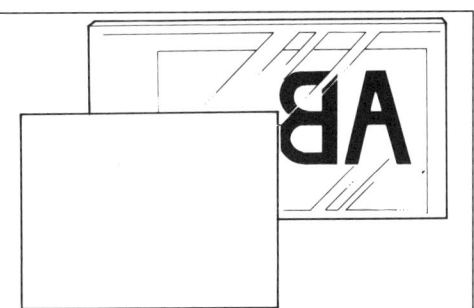

The letter **A** looks the same.
The letter **B** is backwards.

What happens to the other letters of the alphabet?
Which letters do you think look the same?

....

Now look in a mirror. Were you right?

What happens to small letters and numbers in a mirror?

Ivan Idea is a spy. Help him find the secret tape.

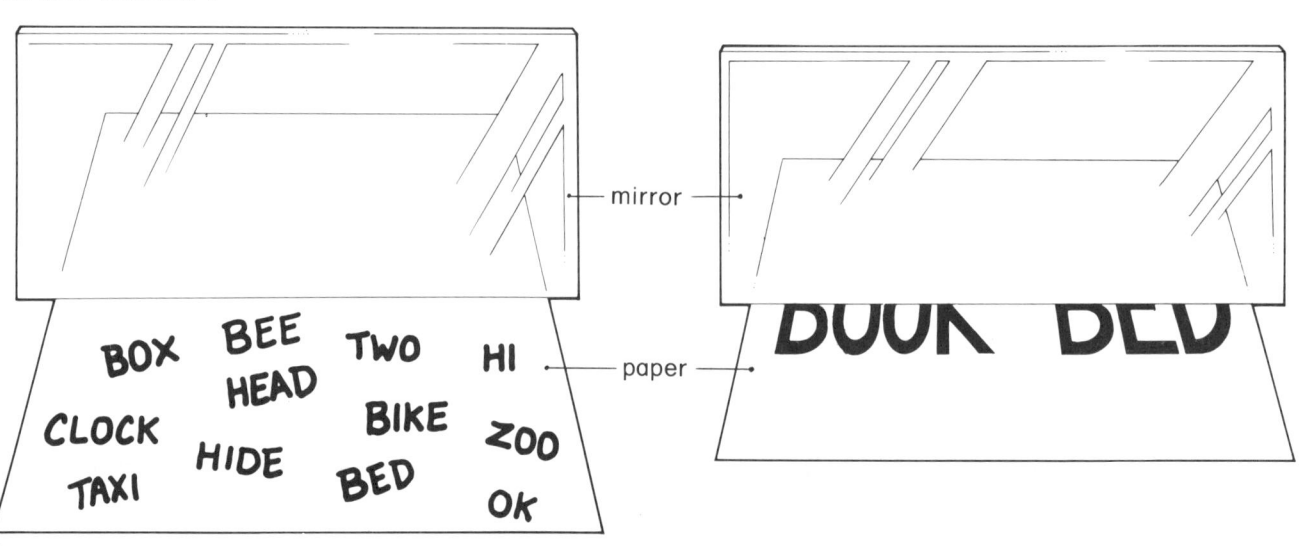

TOP SECRET

There are six tapes in the room.
The secret tape isn't on the bookcase.
It isn't next to the computer.
It isn't behind the clock.
It isn't under the rug and it isn't between the plants.

Can you find the secret tape?

Mirror Puzzles

1 Which words look the same in the mirror?

mirror

paper

BOX BEE TWO HI
HEAD
CLOCK HIDE BIKE ZOO
TAXI BED OK

2 Complete these words.

mirror

paper

BOOK BED

Opposites

Ivan Idea wants to go home.

He has got this secret map, but he doesn't understand it.
He is listening to the secret tape.
Listen to the tape and help Ivan Idea.
Where does he go next?

To the ....

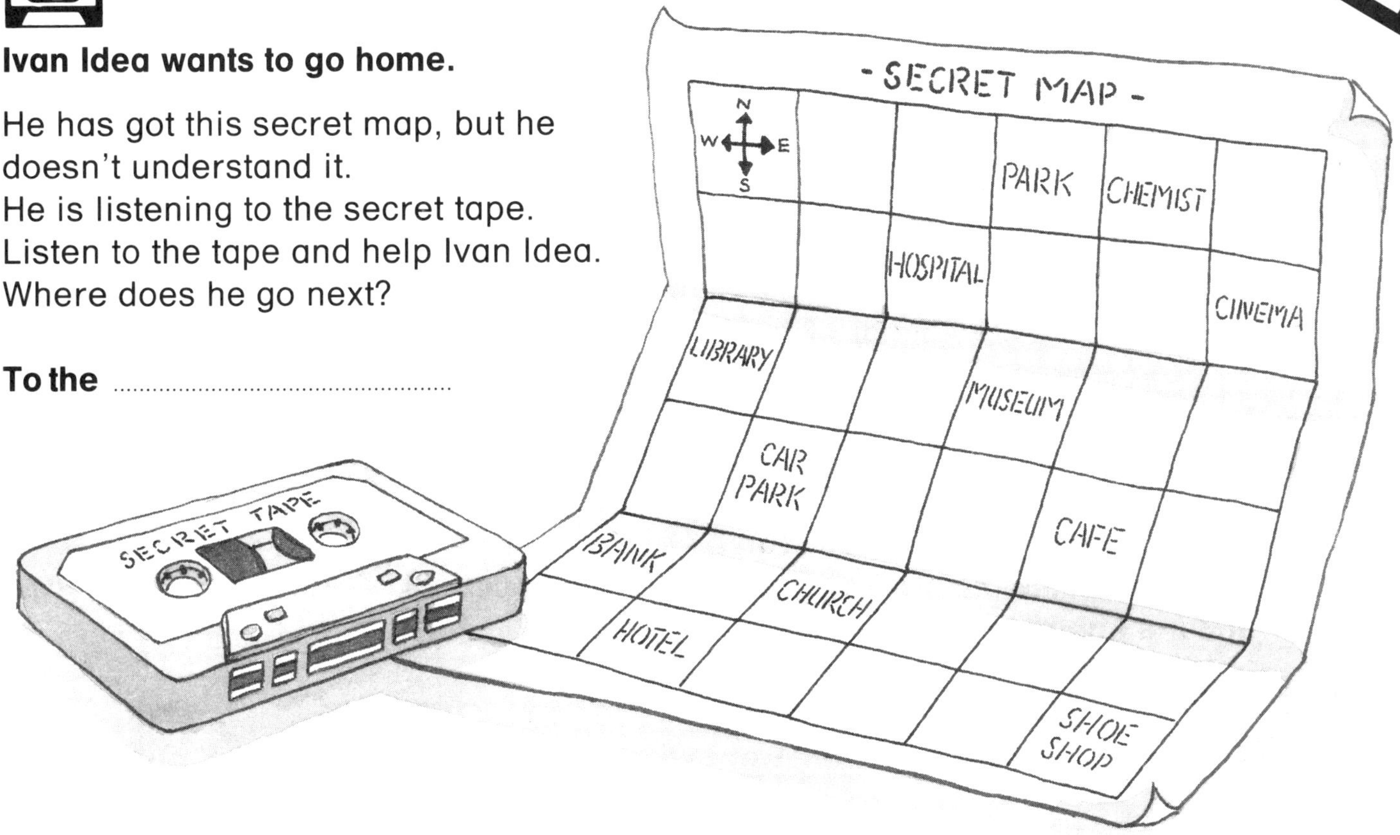

- SECRET MAP -

N W E S

			PARK	CHEMIST	
HOSPITAL					
LIBRARY					CINEMA
			MUSEUM		
CAR PARK				CAFE	
BANK		CHURCH			
HOTEL					SHOE SHOP

thick/thin	empty/full	hot/cold	clean/dirty	light/dark

She's got long .... hair. She's wearing a .... grey coat. Her shoes are .... She's drinking a .... drink and reading a .... book.

He's got short .... hair. He's wearing a .... grey coat and his shoes are .... He's drinking a .... drink and his glass is .... He's reading a .... book.

4

Listen to the second secret message. Help Ivan Idea find the next clue.

The first word is on an empty/full glass. The second word is on a bottle/cup.
The bottle/cup is dark/light green. The third word is on a book/newspaper.
The book/newspaper is on the floor/table next to the spy with the clean/dirty
shoes. The fourth and last word is on a book. The book is thick/thin. It is on the
table next to a hot/cold drink.

Now look at the picture on page 8 of your Coursebook. What is the message?

....

**Now look at the picture on page 9 of your Coursebook. Can you help Ivan Idea
find the numbers?**

Write the numbers here. ....

Add up the numbers. The answer is the same as Ivan Idea's ticket number.

BOAT
ONE ADULT
TICKET NUMBER – **67**

TRAIN
ONE ADULT
TICKET NUMBER –**120**

AEROPLANE
ONE ADULT
TICKET NUMBER – **23**

BUS
ONE ADULT
TICKET NUMBER –**112**

How does Ivan Idea get home?   **By** ....

 **Now that Ivan Idea knows how to get home he needs a passport.**

PASSPORT

signature *Ivan O. Idea*

Name *Ivan O. Idea* ....

Address ....

Town ....

Nationality ....

Height ....

Weight ....

Colour of hair ....

Colour of eyes ....

Passport number ....

This is your passport. Fill in the information.

PASSPORT

STICK PHOTO HERE

signature ....

Name ....

Address ....

Town ....

Nationality ....

Height ....

Weight ....

Colour of hair ....

Colour of eyes ....

Passport number ....

Opposites

a

It looks like a giraffe but it hasn't got a long neck. ☐	It looks like a giraffe but it's got stripes and a short tail. ☐
It looks like a zebra but it's got spots. ☐	It looks like a hippo and an elephant. It's got a hippo's body and an elephant's head. ☐
It looks like a hippo but it's got a long neck and big ears. ☐	It looks like a panda but it's got a very long tail and black and white stripes. ☐

b

c

d

e

f

Draw your animal here.

....
....
....
....
....
....
....
....
....

Tongue Twister

She saw six ships sailing on the sea

Listen to the tape. Write the words and numbers.

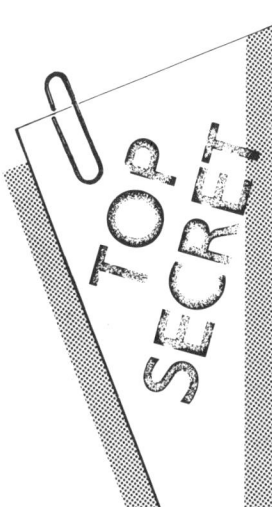

TOP SECRET

Name ....   Nationality ....

Address ....   Eye colour ....

....   Hair colour ....

....   Height ....

Telephone   Age..............................
number ....

Clever Trevor and Jane Brain are spies. Trevor is from the USA and Jane is from Britain. Trevor is two years older than Jane. He is forty-two. But Jane is the tallest. She is 10 cm taller than Trevor. She is 1 m 52.

They always wear long dark coats and hats. Trevor's coat is brown and Jane's is black. Trevor has got short blonde hair and blue eyes. Jane has got long dark hair and her eyes are the same colour as Trevor's.

1 Where is Jane from?

2 Is Trevor British or American?

3 Is Jane older than Trevor?

4 How old is Jane?

5 Who's the tallest, Jane or Trevor?

6 What colour is Trevor's coat?

7 How tall is Trevor?

8 Is Trevor taller than Jane?

9 What colour are Jane's eyes?

10 Who's got the longest hair?

5

 Write a sentence about each picture.

Example:  *The apple is bigger than the tomato.*

| 1 | 2 | 3 | 4 |

Example:  *The ghost is under the table.*

| 5 | 6 | 7 | 8 |

Write the opposite of these words.

Example:
man – *woman*

hello big
  old
 first right
  fat
full
 yes always
tallest girl
 south

Write three sentences about this picture.

Time

What do you need to answer these questions?

1 What day is it today? ....

2 How tall are you? ....

3 What did you do yesterday? ....

4 How long is your pencil? ....

5 What time is it? ....

6 How long does it take to run 100 metres? ....

a a calendar

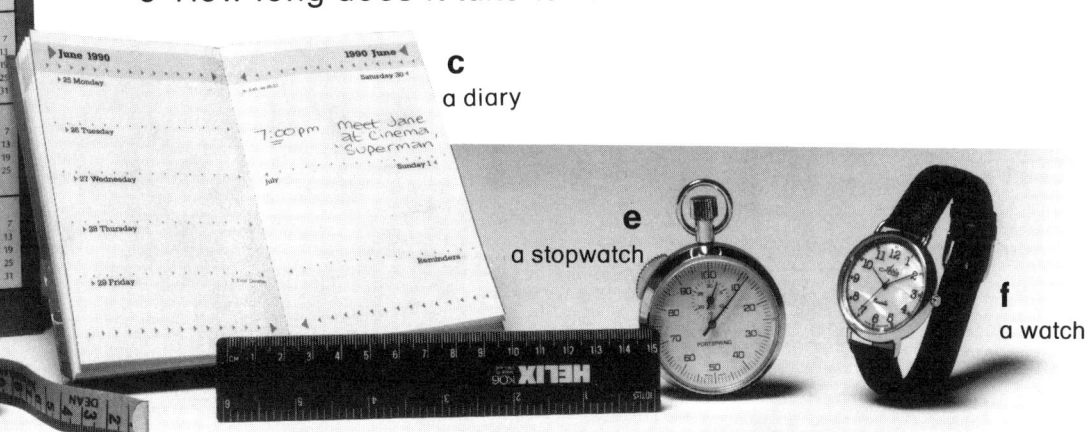

c a diary

e a stopwatch

f a watch

b a tape measure

d a ruler

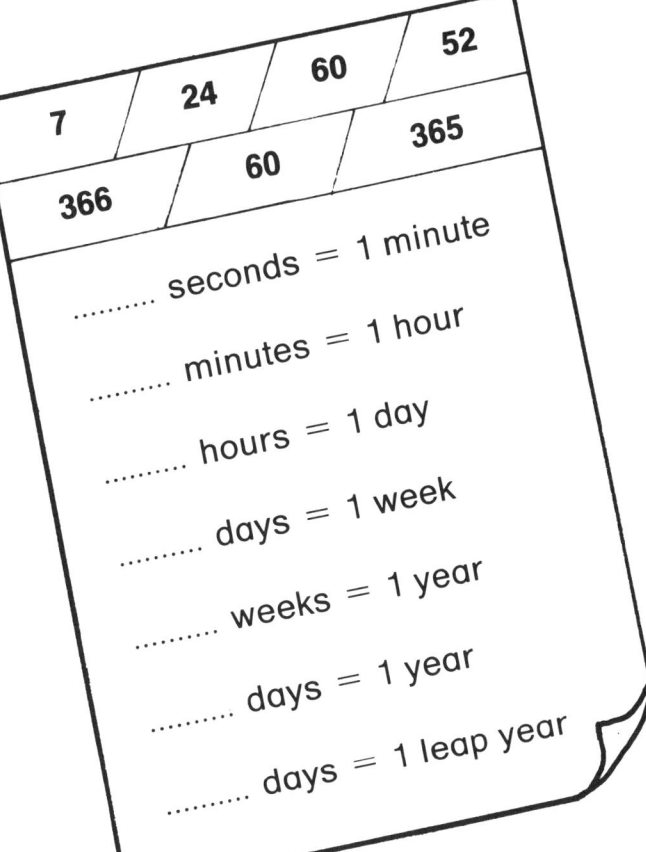

.... seconds = 1 minute

.... minutes = 1 hour

.... hours = 1 day

.... days = 1 week

.... weeks = 1 year

.... days = 1 year

.... days = 1 leap year

7	24	60	52
366	60		365

Draw your watch or your friend's watch.

Answer these questions in your exercise book.
How many clocks are there in your house?
Which rooms are they in?
How many people in your family have got a watch?
Now describe your mother's or father's watch.

	11·42	*It's nearly quarter to twelve.*
	3·14	
	7·35	
	5·28	
	12·59	

What time is it? Draw the hands on the clocks.

The crossword spells out: what time is it

What **day** were you born?

I don't know. But I was born on the 10th of May 1979.

Right, let's find out the day.

1 Start with the last two numbers of the year.	1979	=	79
2 Divide this number by 4.	79 ÷ 4	=	19
3 Now add these two numbers	79 + 19	=	98
4 Add the date of the month.	98 + 10	=	108

5 For January add 1 (0 for a leap year).
For February add 4 (3 for a leap year).
For March and November add 4.
For April and July add 0.
For May add 2.   108 + 2 = 110
For June add 5.
For August add 3.
For September and December add 6.
For October add 1.

6 Divide by 7. What number is left over?   110 ÷ 7 = 15 (5 left over)
1 = Sunday   2 = Monday 3 = Tuesday 4 = Wednesday
5 = Thursday 6 = Friday   0 = Saturday   10th May 1979 = <u>Thursday</u>

What day were you born? Find out!

Time

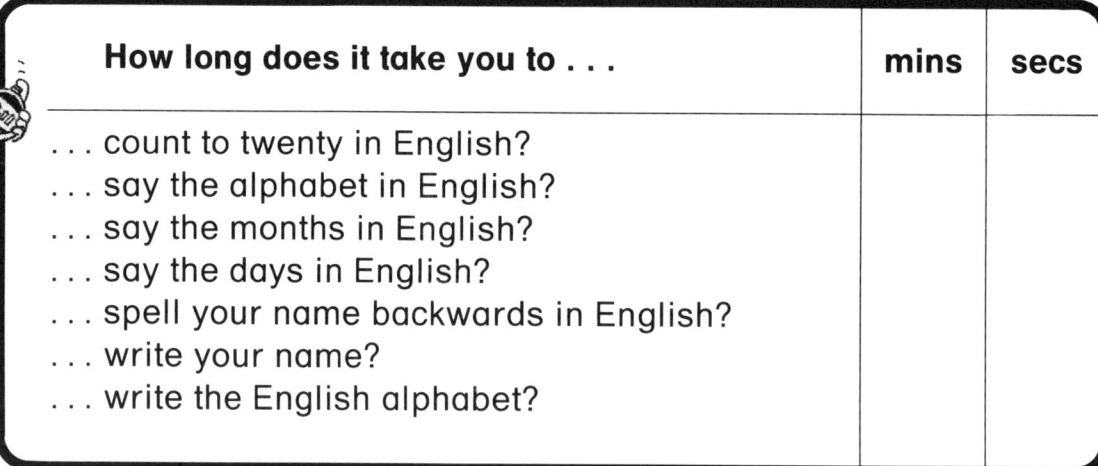

Ready... steady... GO !

How long does it take you to . . .	mins	secs
. . . count to twenty in English?		
. . . say the alphabet in English?		
. . . say the months in English?		
. . . say the days in English?		
. . . spell your name backwards in English?		
. . . write your name?		
. . . write the English alphabet?		

It takes me _____ seconds to count to twenty in English.

....

....

....

....

....

Mark gets up at seven o'clock. It takes him two minutes to get dressed. Then he has a wash and cleans his teeth. That takes him five minutes. Next he eats his breakfast. That takes him fifteen minutes. He watches TV for twelve minutes. Then he puts on his coat, but he can't find his shoes. It takes him five minutes to find them. Finally, Mark leaves his house and walks slowly to school. It takes him twenty minutes.

What time does he get to school? ....

School starts at five to nine. Is he early or late? ....

Read the story on page 20.
Put the pictures in the right order. Write the time on the clocks.

Hurry up! It's time for breakfast.

How long does it take you to get ready for school?

How long does it take you to . . .
        . . . get dressed?
        . . . get washed?
        . . . clean your teeth?
        . . . eat your breakfast?
        . . . get to school?

Guess	Check

Were you right? Find out how long these things take tomorrow morning.

Maureen's Morning
Look at the pictures on page 14 of your Coursebook. Write the story.

Maureen got up at five to seven. Then she

7

Write about what you did this morning.

My Morning

Think about these things.

1 What time did you get up?

2 What did you do first/second?

3 What did you wear?

4 What did you have for breakfast?

5 How long did it take you to eat breakfast?

6 What time did you leave your house?

7 What time did you get to school?

ABCEJLMN OPRSTUY

You can spell the names of six months of the year with these 15 letters.
Which months can you spell?
Which months can't you spell?

Colour the letters to find the days of the week.

E	F	T	N	Z	P	C	Z	U	J	P	V	E	B	K	C	V	Z	G	Z	P	J
S	P	B	Q	L	G	X	B	Q	Z	B	J	U	Q	X	K	C	J	X	Q	C	V
Y	A	W	V	D	R	O	G	A	J	U	N	I	L	Y	R	D	B	L	E	B	D
M	J	G	K	U	J	H	V	T	C	A	C	R	K	S	Z	Y	Z	C	A	G	A
T	Q	B	X	A	Z	P	K	D	L	S	D	Y	X	D	S	D	A	V	Y	A	S
C	V	K	P	Q	L	B	P	X	G	X	L	Q	P	B	Z	K	L	G	K	X	Y
L	J	B	V	G	P	V	C	J	K	B	Q	G	L	X	J	C	K	Q	Y	N	D

Time

 **Three children describe a typical day. What do they do?**
Listen to the tape and write the times.

What and When?	1	2	3	My Day
get up	8.05			
get washed				
clean my teeth				
get dressed				
have a bath				
have breakfast				
comb my hair				
go to school				
have lunch				
finish school				
play football				
play tennis				
play volleyball				
play with friends				
do my homework				
write a letter				
draw and paint				
have dinner				
clean my room				
wash up				
watch TV				
read a book				
go swimming				
go to bed				

Write about what you did yesterday.

A.M.	**My Day** ☆☆) ☆ P.M.

What did you do last week?

	Midnight											Midday											Midnight
	12	1	2	3	4	5	6	7	8	9	10	11	12	1	2	3	4	5	6	7	8	9	10	11	12
Monday																							
Tuesday																							
Wednesday																							
Thursday																							
Friday																							
Saturday																							
Sunday																							

Now answer these questions about yourself. Then ask your friends.

How many hours do you sleep each week? ....

How many hours are you awake? ....

How many hours do you spend at school? ....

How many hours are you awake and not at school? ....

How many hours do you watch TV? ....

What else do you do?

My Diary

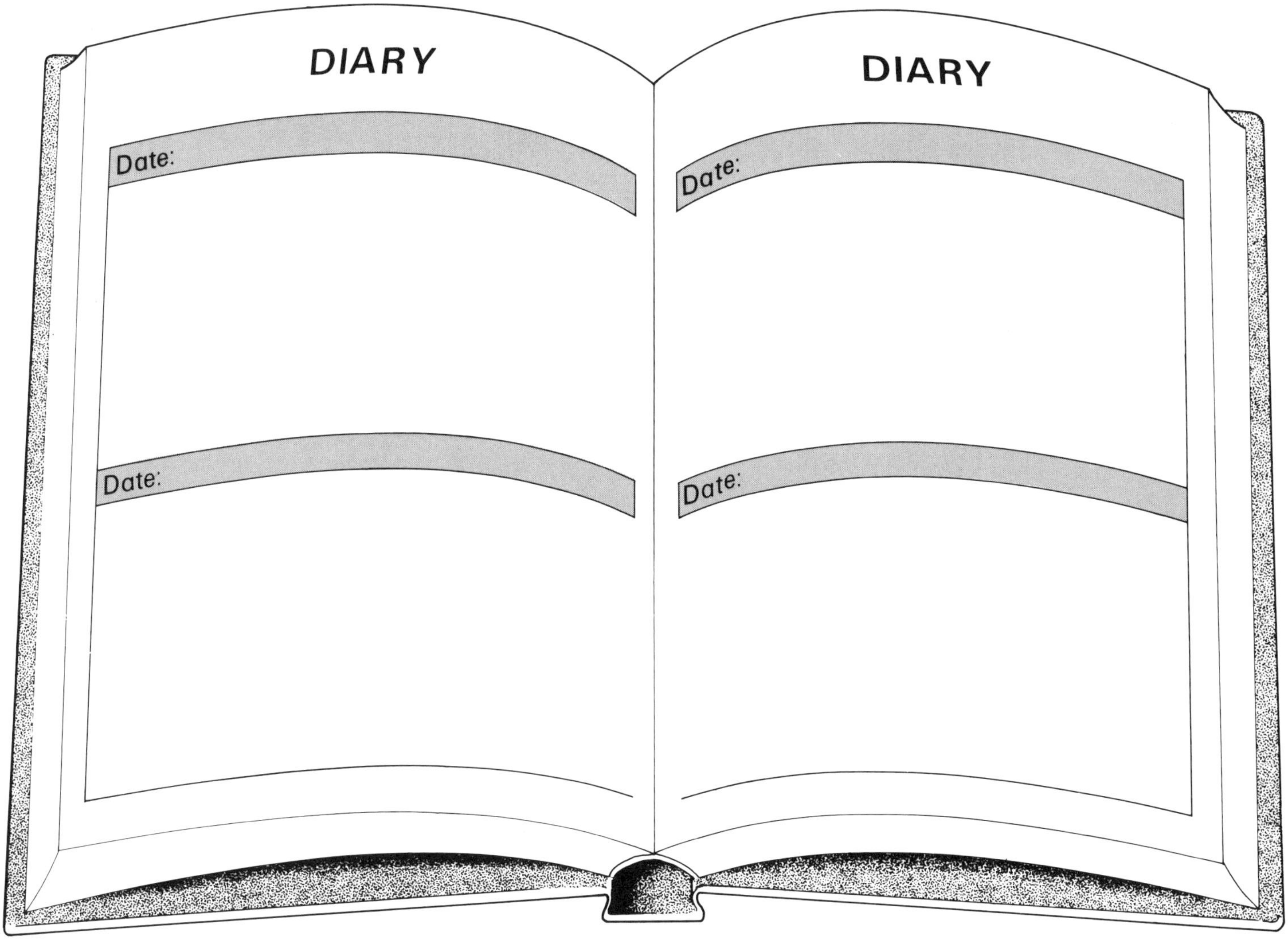

DIARY

Date:

Date:

DIARY

Date:

Date:

Time

Past, present or future? Guess the year.

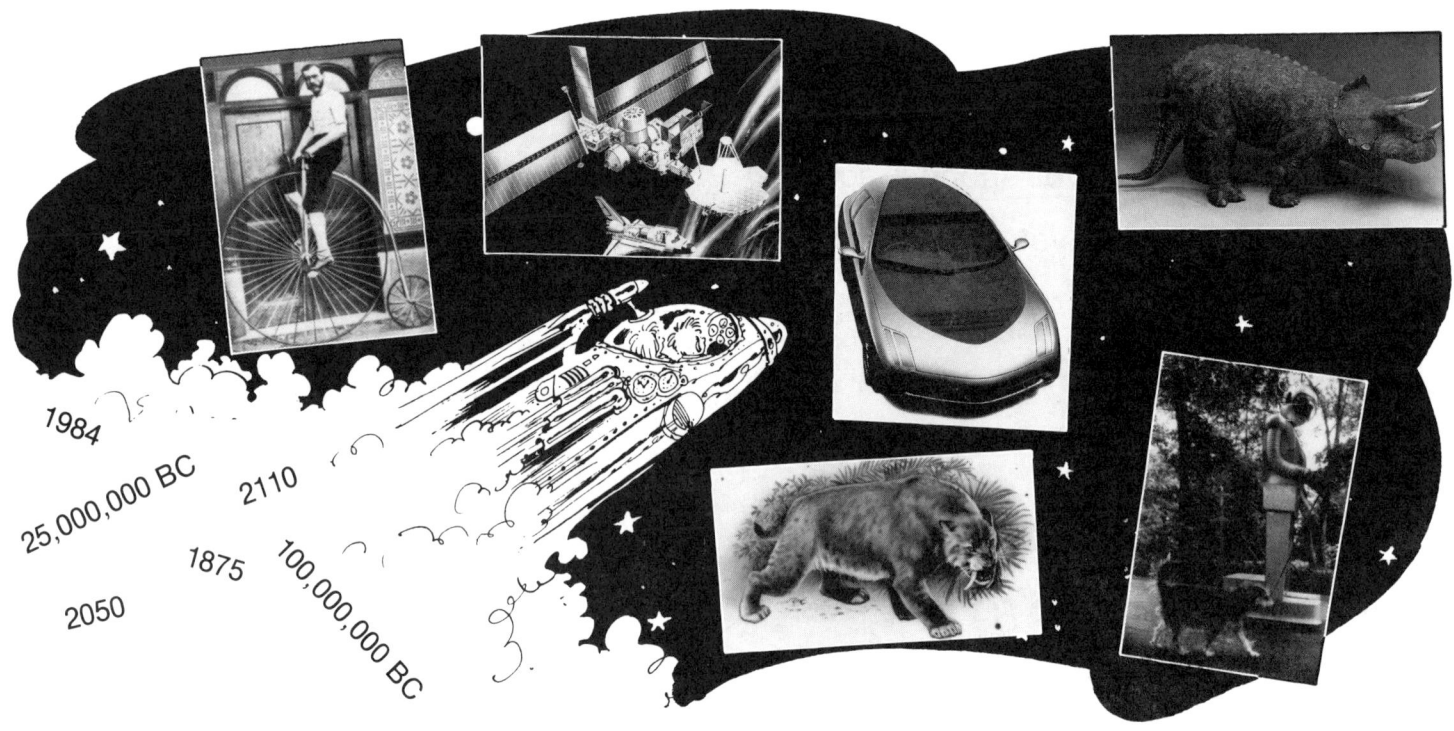

1984

25,000,000 BC

2110

1875

2050

100,000,000 BC

Look at the map on pages 18 and 19 of your Coursebook.

Mr Trip started his journey in London. He went to New York by plane. It took .... hours. Then he went to Acapulco by bus. It took .... hours. From Acapulco he went to Sydney by boat. That took .... hours. Then he went to Tokyo by plane which took .... hours. And finally he went from Tokyo to London by bus. That took .... hours.

How many hours did it take to go around the world? ....

How many days? ....

What does this mean?

26

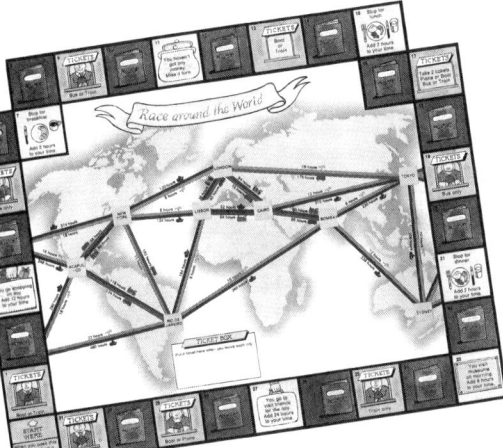

9

Race Around the World

Make eight travel tickets to play the game on pages
18 and 19 of your Coursebook.
Cut out eight pieces of card 6 cm × 3 cm.
Draw a picture and write the words on the card.
Colour the plane tickets red, the boat tickets blue,
the train tickets brown and the bus tickets green.

Now play the game. Where did you go?

			Extra Time
From _London_ to .... by .... It took .... hours.
From .... to .... by .... It took .... hours.
From .... to .... by .... It took .... hours.
From .... to .... by .... It took .... hours.
From .... to .... by .... It took .... hours.
From .... to .... by .... It took .... hours.
From .... to .... by .... It took .... hours.
From .... to .... by .... It took .... hours.
From .... to .... by .... It took .... hours.
From .... to .... by .... It took .... hours.

Total .... **hours**

Where did you go? Write a postcard to your friend.

Dear

....

....

....

....

1 What are these?

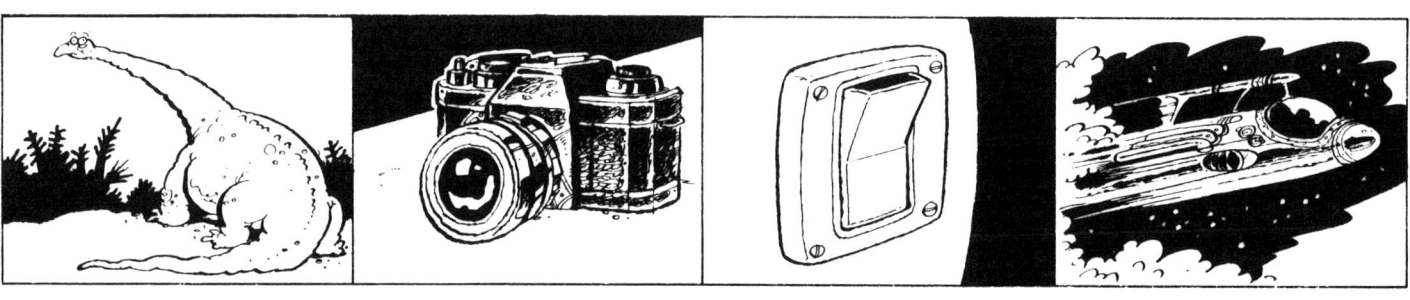

....

2 Find a word which rhymes with these words.

now   then   snow   June   head   crunch   Jean

....

3 Put these sentences in the correct order.

"Look out! It's moving," his sister said.

"Come on. Let's go!" he said to Jean.

Jim picked up his camera and jumped out of the machine.

And looked at Jim and thought, "That's lunch!"

A hundred, a thousand, a million years or more,

And with a click of the switch she started the machine.

The dinosaur walked with a thud and a crunch,

"Be careful! It's dangerous!" shouted sister Jean.

Jim ran quickly back to the machine.

Jim pointed his camera at a dinosaur's head,

They stopped in the time of the dinosaur.

Time

Read the poem. Find a word which means the same as:

1 very fast ....

2 more than one ....

3 very old ....

Now find the opposite of these words:

1 forwards ....

2 is ....

3 past ....

4 closed ....

5 put down ....

6 slowly ....

7 brother ....

Where did you go in the Time Machine?

....
....
....
....
....
....
....
....
....
....
....
....

Tongue Twister

Please pass Paul the purple book
and blue pen.

Ask your friends: What is the most important day for you?

Names	Most important day	Why?

Plan a birthday party.
Imagine it is your birthday. You are having a party.

1 Design and make an invitation for your friends.

2 How many people are coming to your party?
Make a list.

3 What are you going to eat?
Make a shopping list.

Kim Lee starts school every day at half past eight. Usually he gets up at about seven o'clock, but yesterday he got up at quarter past seven. Usually he walks to school, but sometimes he goes by bus. He went by bus yesterday. He got to school at twenty-five past eight. School finishes at four o'clock every day. But on Monday and Wednesday Kim stays at school to play football. He plays for ninety minutes then he goes home.

1 What time does Kim Lee start school?
2 What time did he get up yesterday?
3 What time did he get to school?
4 Was he early or late?
5 Did he walk to school or go by bus yesterday?
6 What time does school finish?
7 What does Kim do on Mondays and Wednesdays?
8 What time does Kim go home on Mondays and Wednesdays?

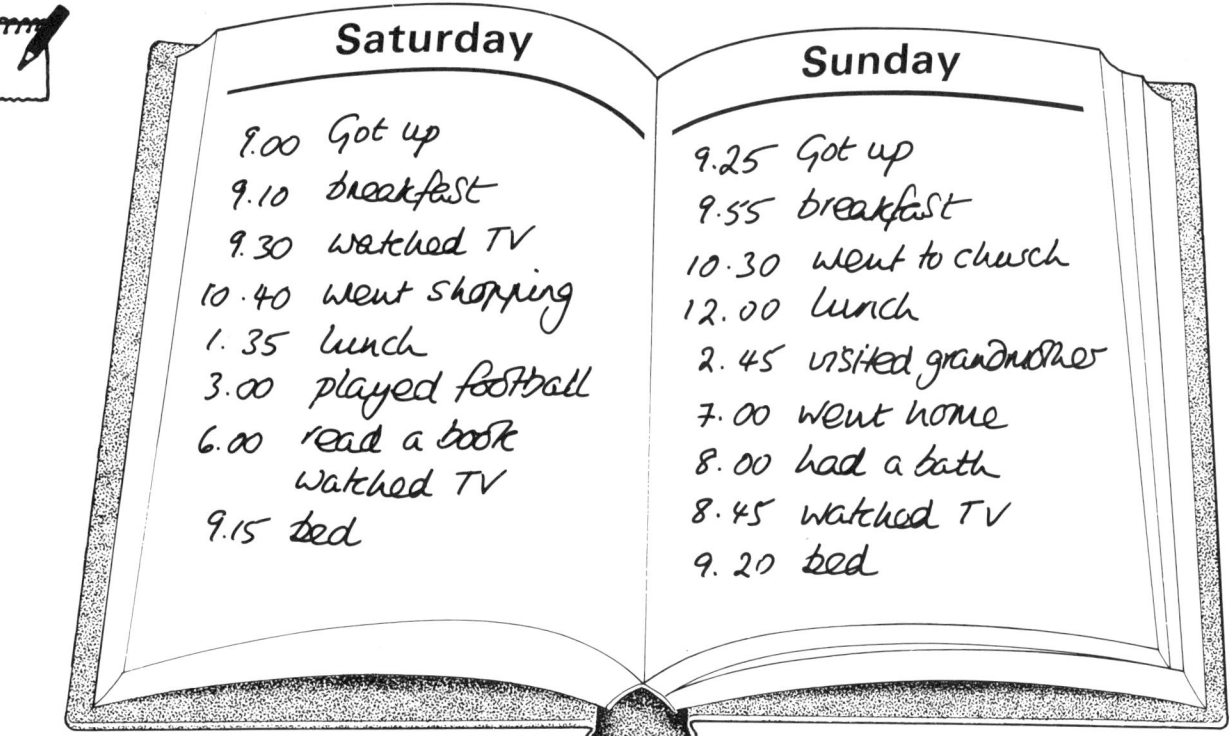

Saturday	
8.00	Got up
9.10	breakfast
9.30	watched TV
10.40	went shopping
1.35	lunch
3.00	played football
6.00	read a book
	watched TV
9.15	bed

Sunday	
9.25	Got up
9.55	breakfast
10.30	went to church
12.00	lunch
2.45	visited grandmother
7.00	went home
8.00	had a bath
8.45	watched TV
9.20	bed

On Saturday Bill got up at nine o'clock and then had his breakfast at ten past nine. At half past nine he watched TV and at twenty to eleven he went shopping. He had lunch at twenty-five to two and at three o'clock he played football. In the evening he read a book and watched TV. He went to bed at quarter past nine.

What did Bill do on Sunday?

Senses

 **Look at the picture on page 22 of your Coursebook.**

1 Find four things that can fly. What are they? Where are they?
2 Find three things that are dangerous. Why are they dangerous?
3 How many animals can you see in the park?
4 How many boys are wearing red T-shirts?
5 Can you find six numbers hidden in the picture?
6 Can you find someone looking at a bird?
7 Can you find someone listening to music?
8 Can you find someone eating something? What does it taste like?
9 Can you find someone smelling something? What does it smell like?
10 Can you find someone touching something? What does it feel like?

Make a list of things in the park that you can see, hear, touch, taste and smell.

see	hear	touch	taste	smell

Look at these pictures. What do you think they are?

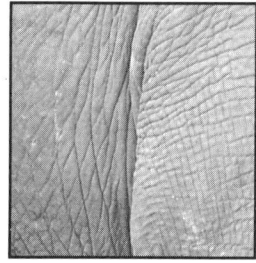 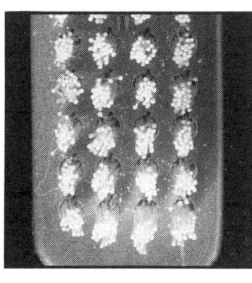 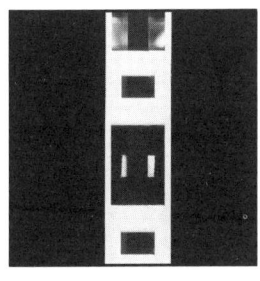 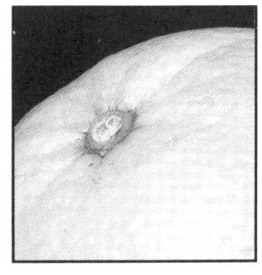 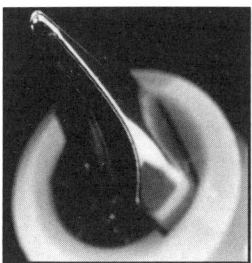

1 .... 2 .... 3 .... 4 .... 5 ....

 **Now listen to the people talking. What words do they use?**
Put a ✓ in the box next to the words each time you hear them.

	1	2	3	4	5
I don't know.					
I've no idea.					
I haven't got a clue.					
I'm not sure.					
Maybe it's . . .					
I think it's . . .					
It looks like . . .					
Do you think . . .?					
What do you think . . .?					

 **Now it's your turn. What do you think these are?**

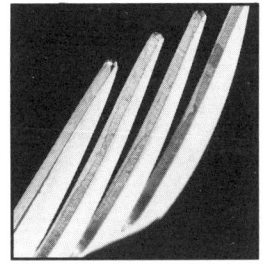    

11

| I know! It's . . . | I haven't got a clue! | It tastes like . . . | It looks like . . . |
| No, I don't think it's . . . | It smells like . . . | What is it? | Maybe it's . . . |

| SIGHT | SOUND | TOUCH | TASTE | SMELL |
| look | | | | |

look bee food listen drink TV cheese sock pick up see music hear

34

Senses

Can you do these things without looking?

	Me	My friend
Write your name.		
Write the alphabet in a straight line.		
Draw a house.		
Stand on one leg and turn around three times.		
Say what is on page 6 of your Coursebook.		
Open your Coursebook at page 40.		

How are they feeling? Draw the faces.

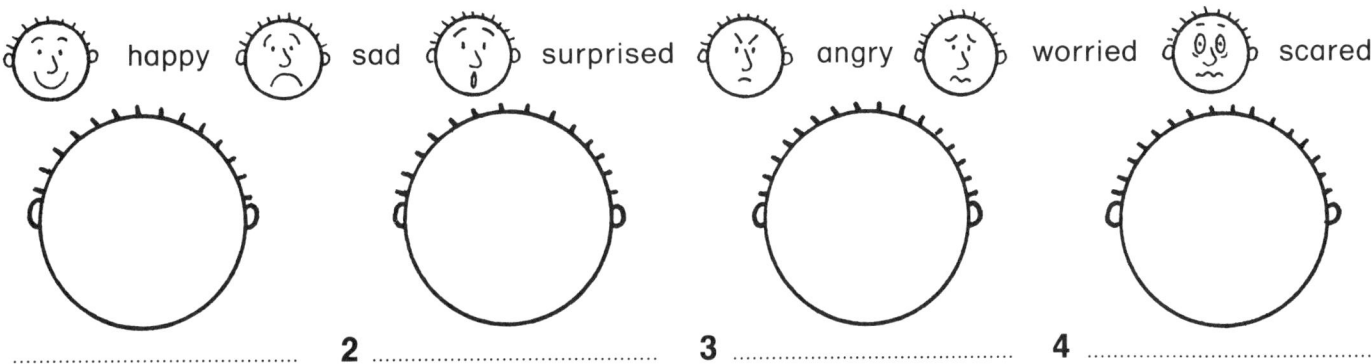

happy   sad   surprised   angry   worried   scared

1 .... 2 .... 3 .... 4 ....

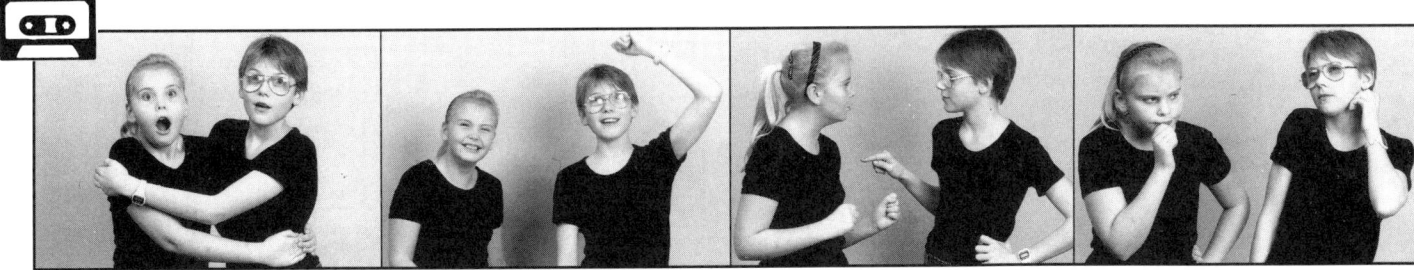

A They are scared   **B** They are happy   **C** They are angry   **D** They are puzzled

1
▲ Hey, that's my pen.
● No, it isn't. It's mine.
▲ This is yours. That's mine.
● No, it isn't.
▲ Yes, it is.

2
▲ Come on. Let's go in.
● I'm not going in there!
▲ Why not?
● I'm scared. Look at that huge dog!
▲ Oh yes.

3
▲ Who won the football match?
● We did. We won.
▲ What was the score?
● 10-0.

4
▲ What's that?
● It's a cat, I think.
▲ Well, why is it chasing that dog?
● I haven't got a clue!

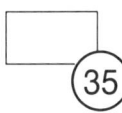

WHAT AM I SAYING ?
WATCH MY LIPS.

Work with your friend. Say a word but do NOT make a sound.

1 'Say' some of the words from the lists **A** and **B**.
Can your friend lip-read the words?
Put a ✓ next to the words they get right.
Put a ✗ next to the words they get wrong.
Is it easier to lip-read long words or short words?

2 Now try with words in your own language and words in English. Which are the most difficult to lip-read?

A		B	
bag		banana	
dog		newspaper	
car		potato	
men		elephant	
long		opposite	
six		crocodile	
house		telephone	
dark		dangerous	
game		computer	
why		cardigan	

Make a Magic Bird

You need: 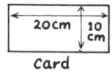 20cm 10cm Card  30cm string  sticky tape Coloured pencils

1 Fold the card in half.

2 Open the card. Draw a bird on one side and a cage, in the same place, on the other side.

3 Turn the card over and tape the string on the back.

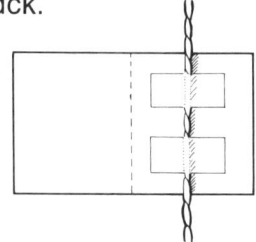

4 Fold the card and tape the two halves together.

5 Roll the string quickly between your finger and thumb. Can you see the bird inside the cage?

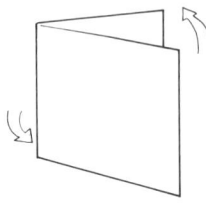

6 Or you could draw a different picture.

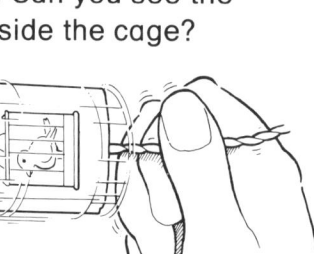

Look at the four pictures for 30 seconds.
What are the differences between the pictures?

What can you see in these pictures? Are you sure? Look again.

How many triangles can you see?

Look at the black squares for a few seconds. What can you see between the squares?

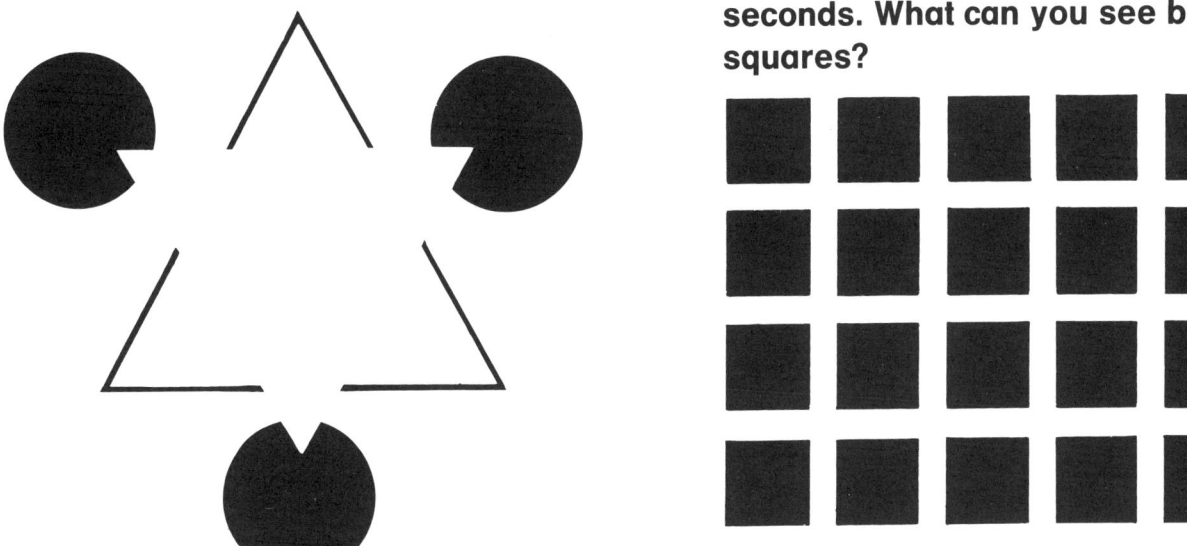

Senses

LISTEN CAREFULLY. WHAT DO YOU THINK IT IS?

How good is your friend's hearing?

1 Choose six objects. Show them to your friend. Put a book between yourself and your friend. Drop each object on the table. Your friend listens. Can they guess the object?

objects	right	wrong

2 Now try listening with only one ear. Is it more difficult?

Sound Code

A	B	C	D	E	F	G	H	I	J	K	L	M

N	O	P	Q	R	S	T	U	V	W	X	Y	Z

A Listen to the tape. What are these words?

1 ____ ____ ____ ____ ____

2 ____ ____ ____ ____ ____ ____

3 ____ ____ ____ ____ ____

4 ____ ____ ____ ____ ____ ____ ____

5 ____ ____ ____ ____

6 ____ ____ ____ ____

B Now you write some words. Say them in code to your friend.

....

....

....

....

....

....

People who can't hear and speak use their hands to talk.
This is called sign language. Here is the alphabet in sign language.

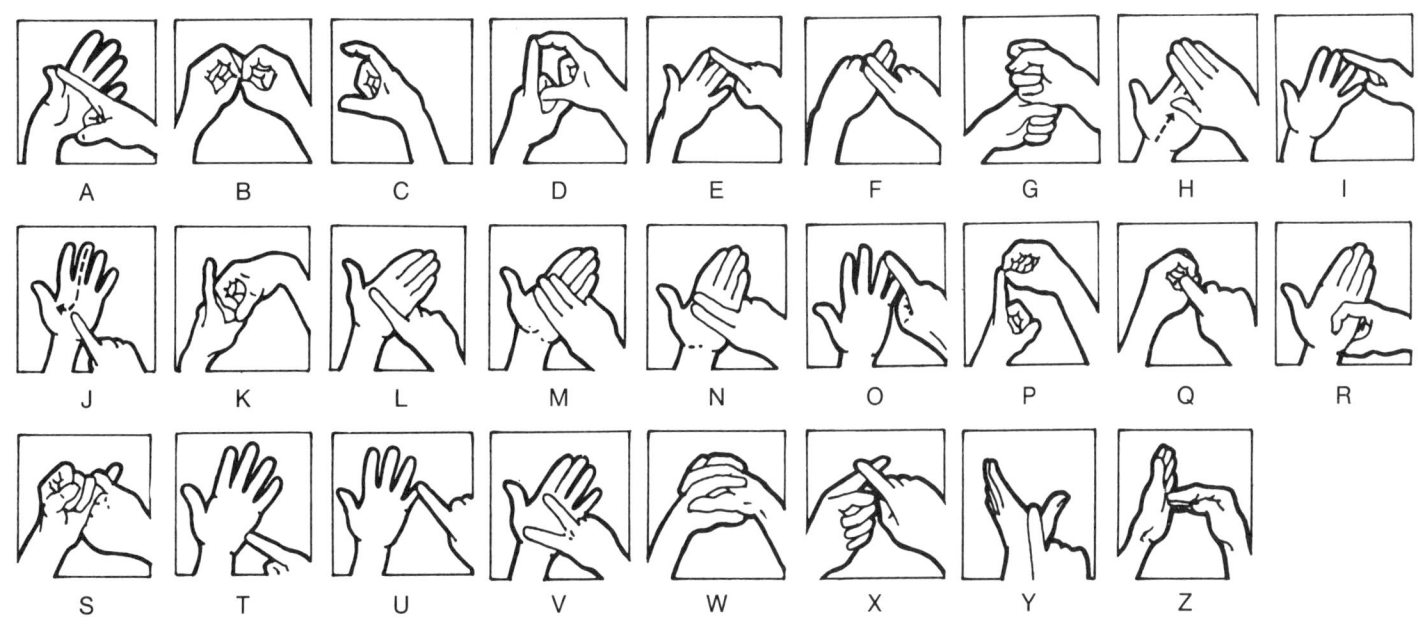

This woman is using the sign language alphabet. What is she saying?

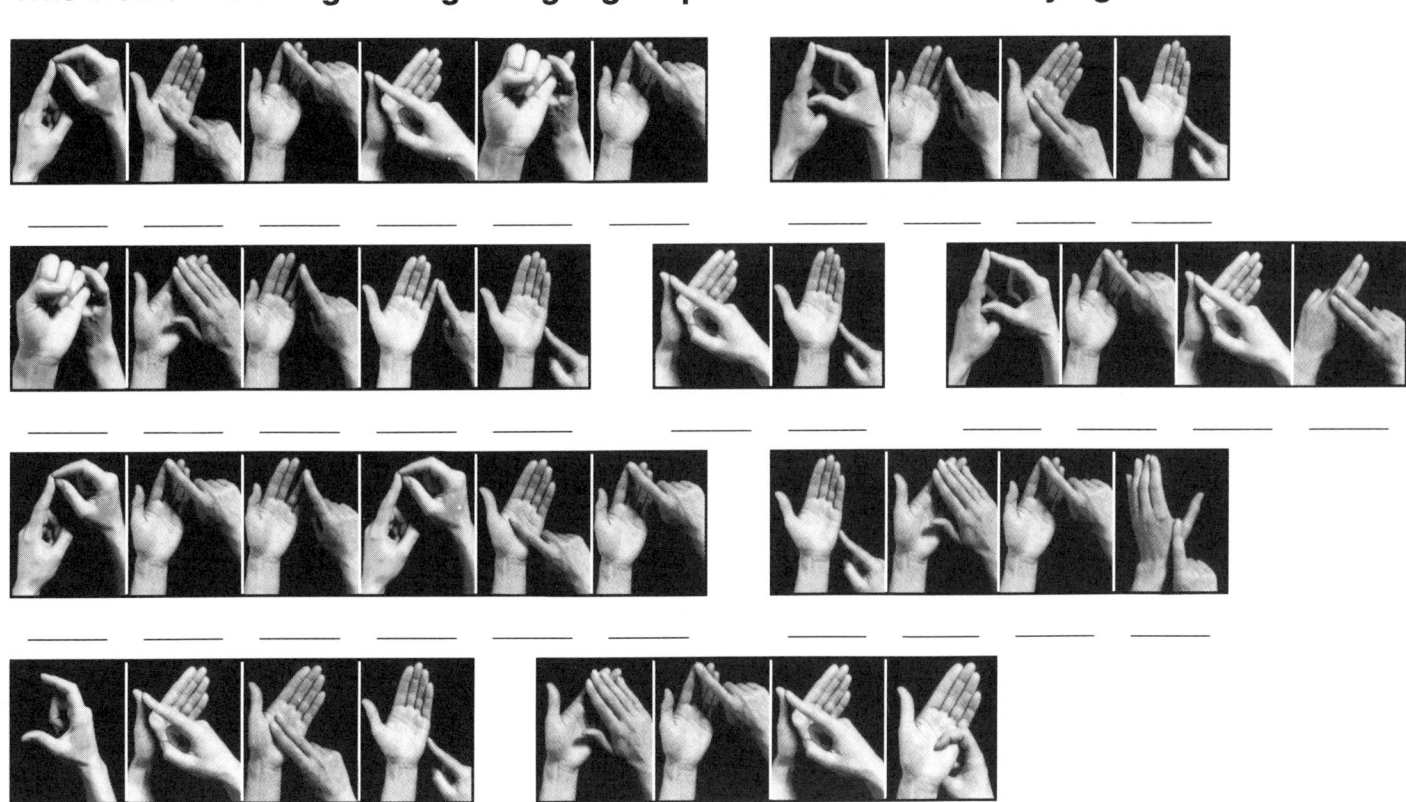

Now you make some words with your hands.

What sound do these animals make?
Put the sound and the animal together.

| woof-woof | cock-a-doodle-do | baa-baa | eek-eek | twit-twoo |

CAN YOU SEE SOUND ?

Work with a friend. You need a paper tissue.

1 Hold the tissue about 10 cm in
front of your face.
Say these words.
How much does the tissue move?
Not at all, a little or a lot?
Put a ✔ in the right box.

Words	Movement		
	none	a little	a lot
bin			
pin			
cat			
spin			
van			
plane			
sea			
hat			
flat			
work			

2 Now try with words in your own language and words in English.
What is the difference?

Senses

1 It feels .... and ....
It's round and it's ....
small.

2 It's .... heavy. It's hard
and .... and ....
big.

3 It's a .... shape. It feels
very soft and light. It's ....
.... big.

4 It's very .... and very
.... It .... quite
smooth and it's sort of square.

5 It .... cold and ....
smooth and ....

6 ....
....
....

Read the poem, 'At the Seaside'. Write the sentence which describes each picture.

I love to feel the sand between my toes.

I love to hear people splashing in the water.

I love the taste and feel of ice-cream on my tongue.

I love to hear the waves crashing on the beach.

I love to feel the sea against my skin when I swim.

....

....

....

....

....

When we touch things we feel the texture. Collect rubbings of different textures.

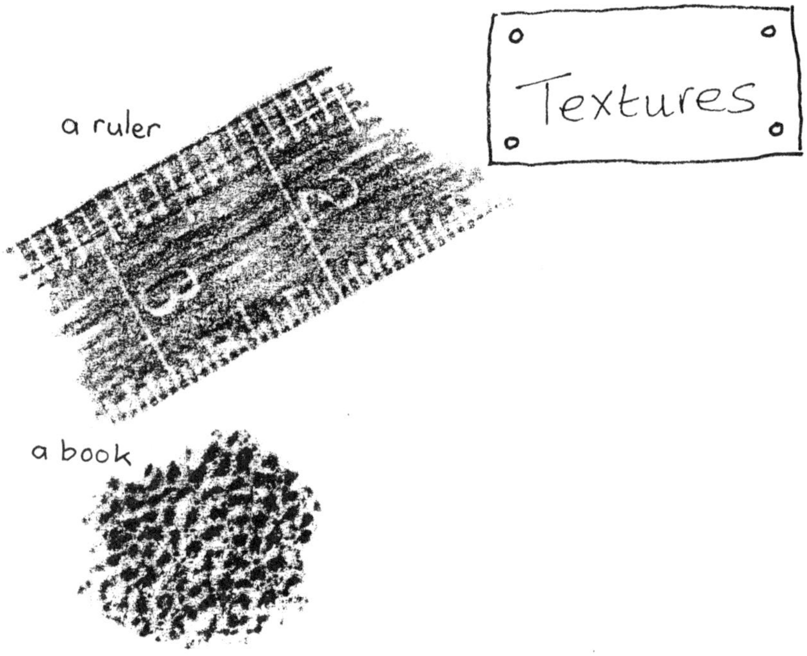

a ruler

Textures

a book

rough	smooth

hard	soft

heavy	light

NO PEEPING!

A **You need:**  thick card  thin card  a pencil  a ruler  scissors  a blindfold

1 Work in groups of four.
Cut these shapes out of the card.
Now blindfold one pupil.
Put the shapes in front of them.
Ask questions, e.g. 'Can you find the small, thin circle?'
How long does it take to find the right shape? Count the seconds.
Is it easier to find big shapes or small shapes, thick shapes or thin shapes?

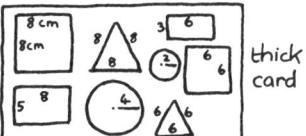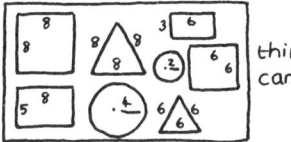

Can you find the big, thick square? Ready, steady, go! One...two...

I think it's this one.

shape	time

2 Try the experiment again wearing gloves. Is it more difficult?
3 Try the experiment again using shapes made from rough and smooth textures.

B **You need:**  card  glue  a brush  sand  a tray  a blindfold

1 Put the card on the tray.
Paint any three letters on the card with glue.
Sprinkle sand over the letters.
Shake off the extra sand on to the tray.
Put the cards on the wall.
Now work in pairs.
Blindfold your friend and ask them to touch the letters.
Can they guess the letters?

B s r

What letter do you think this is?

I think it's a capital 'b'.

letter						
✓ ✗						

2 Try the experiment again using a different finger, your thumb or your other hand. Is it more difficult?

Senses

You need: Small pieces of potato and carrot

1 Work in pairs.
One pupil closes their eyes and holds their nose.
Put a piece of potato or carrot into their mouth.
Can they guess what it is?
Repeat the taste test four more times. Are they always right?

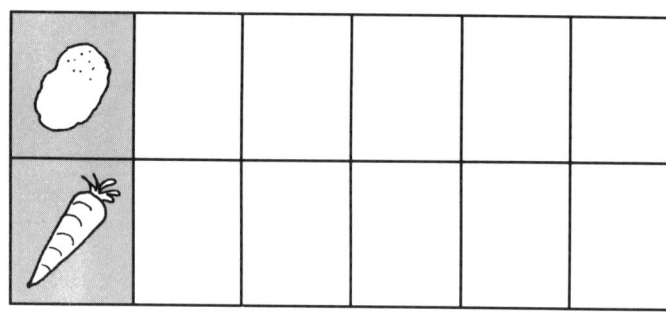

2 Try the experiment again using other food. You could use:

coca-cola v lemonade   an orange v a lemon   sugar v salt

3 Try the experiment again using fruit sweets.

The class needs:  plastic cups    paper tissues    elastic bands   food- e.g. coffee, banana etc.

Write a number on each cup.
Put the food in the cups.
Cover each cup with a tissue and an elastic band.
Work in pairs.
Smell each cup.
What do you think is in the cups?

	Me	My friend
1		
2		
3		
4		
5		
6		

Write the past tense of these words in the crossword.

Down

1 clean
4 like
5 see
6 point
9 eat
10 taste
12 close
14 touch
15 watch
16 look
21 go
23 is

Across

2 make
3 live
6 play
7 say
8 run
11 hear
13 start
17 can
18 take
19 have
20 feel
22 are
24 drink
25 do
26 sit

Clarence the Clown can't climb cliffs.

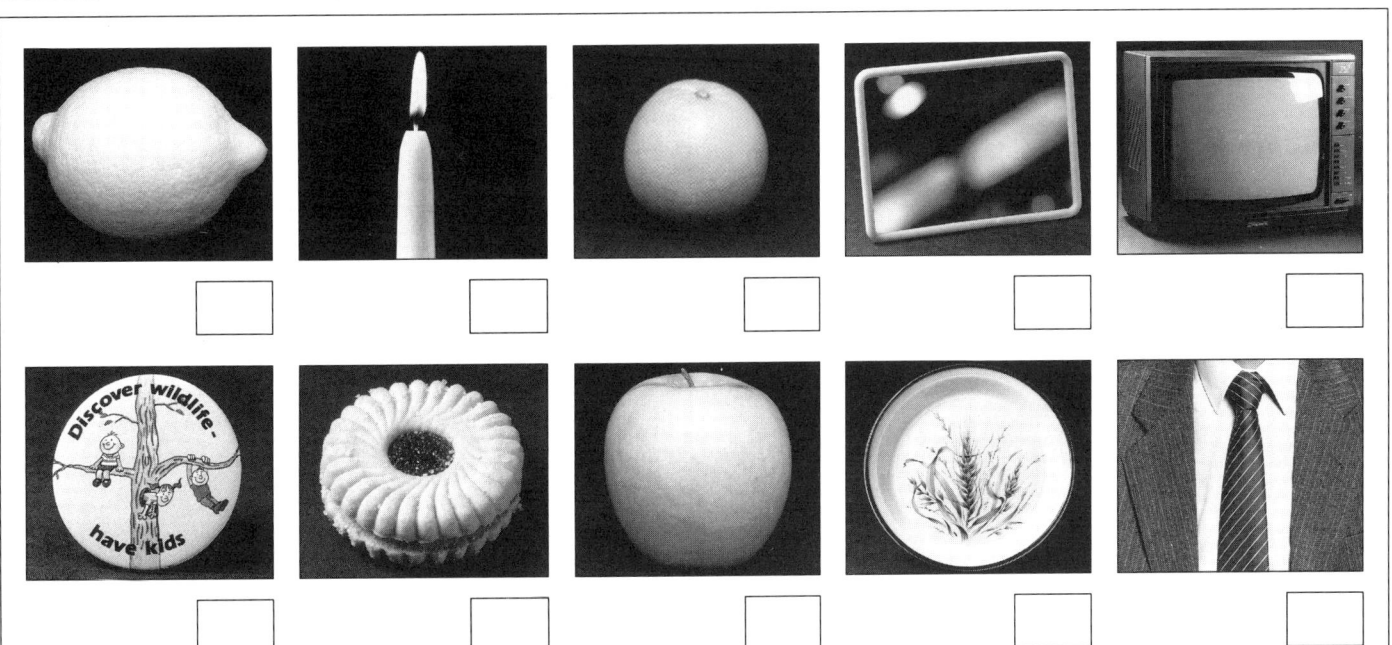

Use your Reader. Are these sentences true or false?

1 Arnold was wearing an old jacket. ☐

2 Arnold saw a girl riding a tiny horse. ☐

3 Arnold saw purple rats. ☐

4 Arnold saw fourteen different animals on the other side of the mirror. ☐

5 Jim and Jean saw a dinosaur. ☐

6 Jim and Jean went to ancient Rome. ☐

7 Jim and Jean went to the past and the future in their Time Machine. ☐

8 All of the boys saw the monster. ☐

9 They looked for the monster in the park. ☐

10 The little boy said that the monster touched him. ☐

 **1 Rearrange the words to make questions.**

Example: smooth Is it rough or?

= *Is it rough or smooth?*

1 it like does look What?

2 that say Can again you?

3 sweet it Does taste?

4 did say you What?

5 happy look or Does sad he?

2

Maybe.	What does it taste like?	Pardon?

No, I don't think it's a vegetable.	I don't know.

Mmm....

GIRL What do you think this is?
BOY   ....
GIRL I said, what do you think this is?
BOY   ....
GIRL Do you think it's a fruit?
BOY   ....
GIRL Or a vegetable?
BOY   ....
GIRL Here, let me taste it.
BOY   ....
GIRL It tastes sweet. Mmm . . . nice!

Nature

Use your Reader. Answer these questions. Find the answers as quickly as possible.

> You don't need to read all the information to find the answers. Look for the most important words.

1 Is a crocodile a reptile? ....

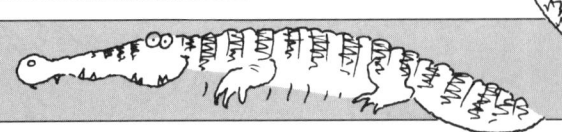

> The most important word in this question is **reptile**.
> Look quickly in your Reader for the word 'reptile'.

2 How many different kinds of mammals are there? ....

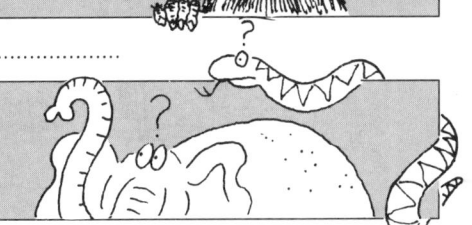

> **How many** tells us to look for a number.
> **Mammal** is the most important word.
> Look under the word 'mammal' for a number.

3 Which group has the biggest animals? ....

> What do you **think** the answer is? Mammal or reptile, maybe?
> Find the section on mammals and check if you are right.
> If you are wrong, look under reptiles.

Now answer these questions. If you think you know the answer, guess then check. If not, what are the most important words?

1 Is a toad an amphibian? ....

2 How many different kinds of reptiles are there? ....

3 Can mammals fly? ....

4 What do birds use their beaks for? ....

1 This animal lives in water but it isn't a fish.

2 An _____ is an arthropod.

3 All birds have a _____ or a bill.

4 Amphibians lay _____ eggs.

5 Mammals have warm _____ .

6 Most mammals have _____ .

7 All birds have _____ .

8 These animals have gills.

9 This animal is a reptile.

10 What are animals without a backbone called?

11 Insects and spiders are _____ .

12 These animals lay hard eggs.

 **Can you find the mistakes in these notes? Listen to the interview.**

tarantula - arthropod (20 legs) - poisonous
eats people
shark - mammal - lives in water - can't breathe
under water - has a beak
octopus - fish - lives in water - usually rivers
polar bear - mammal - eats birds - lives in
hot places - black and white fur
rhino - large reptile - cold blooded -
doesn't like water - eats grass

Describe a whale.

hair

fins

scales

cold-blooded

beak

bill

feathers

wings

fur

gills

bird

can breathe
under water

can swim

fish

Whale

lays soft
eggs

amphibian

mammal

reptile

doesn't lay
eggs

vertebrate

can
fly

warm-blooded

lays hard
eggs

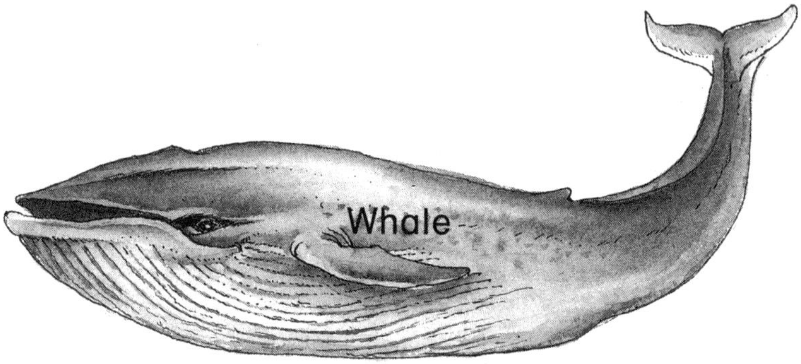

Now describe some other animals that you know.

Draw two animals and write about the differences between them.

What's the difference between a .... and a ....?

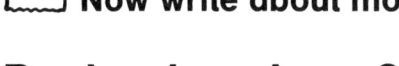 **Now write about more animals in your exercise book.**

Real or imaginary?

Look at these animals and read the descriptions. Some of them are real and some are imaginary. Which ones do you think are real? Are you sure?

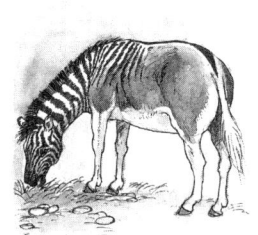 The **Quagga** is now extinct. It was a mammal. It was like a horse and a zebra. It had a zebra's head and neck and a horse's body and legs.

 **Dugongs** live in water but they are mammals. They can be three metres long and they have skin like an elephant.

 A **Duck-billed Platypus** is a mammal but it lays eggs. It has a bill and feet like a bird and it swims like a fish.

 The **Red Uakari** is a small monkey. It is only about half a metre long. It has long brown hair and a red face. It lives in South America.

 The **Amazon Lizard** lives only in Brazil. It is red and green and it grows up to twelve metres long. It eats snakes and fish.

 The **Great White Snail** lived on islands in the Indian Ocean. It was up to three metres long. It had a beautiful white shell. This mollusc is now extinct.

Nature

What do you know about dinosaurs? Are these sentences true or false?

	Guess	Check

Dinosaurs lived 1000 years ago.
All dinosaurs were reptiles.
All dinosaurs ate meat.
All dinosaurs were big.
Some dinosaurs were 27 metres long.

Use your Reader to find out more about prehistoric animals.

	dinosaur	herbivore	carnivore	size (length)	walked on 2 legs	walked on 4 legs
Apatosaurus						
Archaeopteryx						
Compsognathus						
Diplodocus						
Pteranodon						
Tyrannosaurus						

Trace the bones. Cut them out. Build the dinosaur.

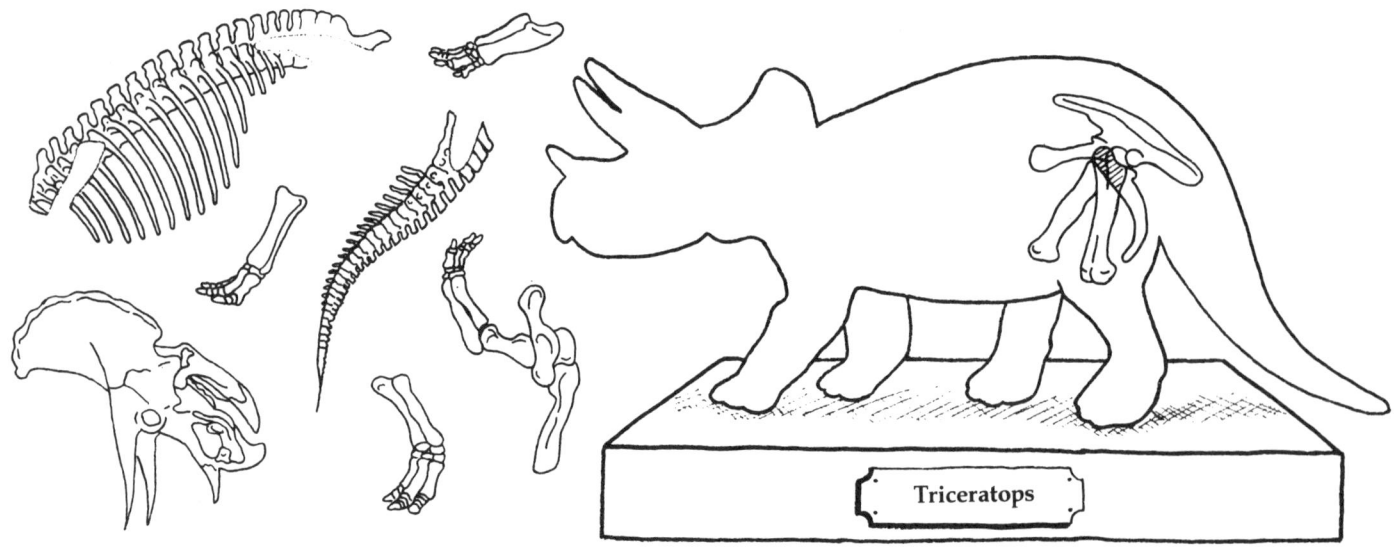

Triceratops

Here is a plan of a museum. The museum is having an exhibition of prehistoric animals. They want to put one skeleton in each room. Use your Reader to find out how long each skeleton is. Which rooms would you put these skeletons in?

Pteranodon	Hypsilophodon	Apatosaurus	Diplodocus	Brachiosaurus	Stegosaurus

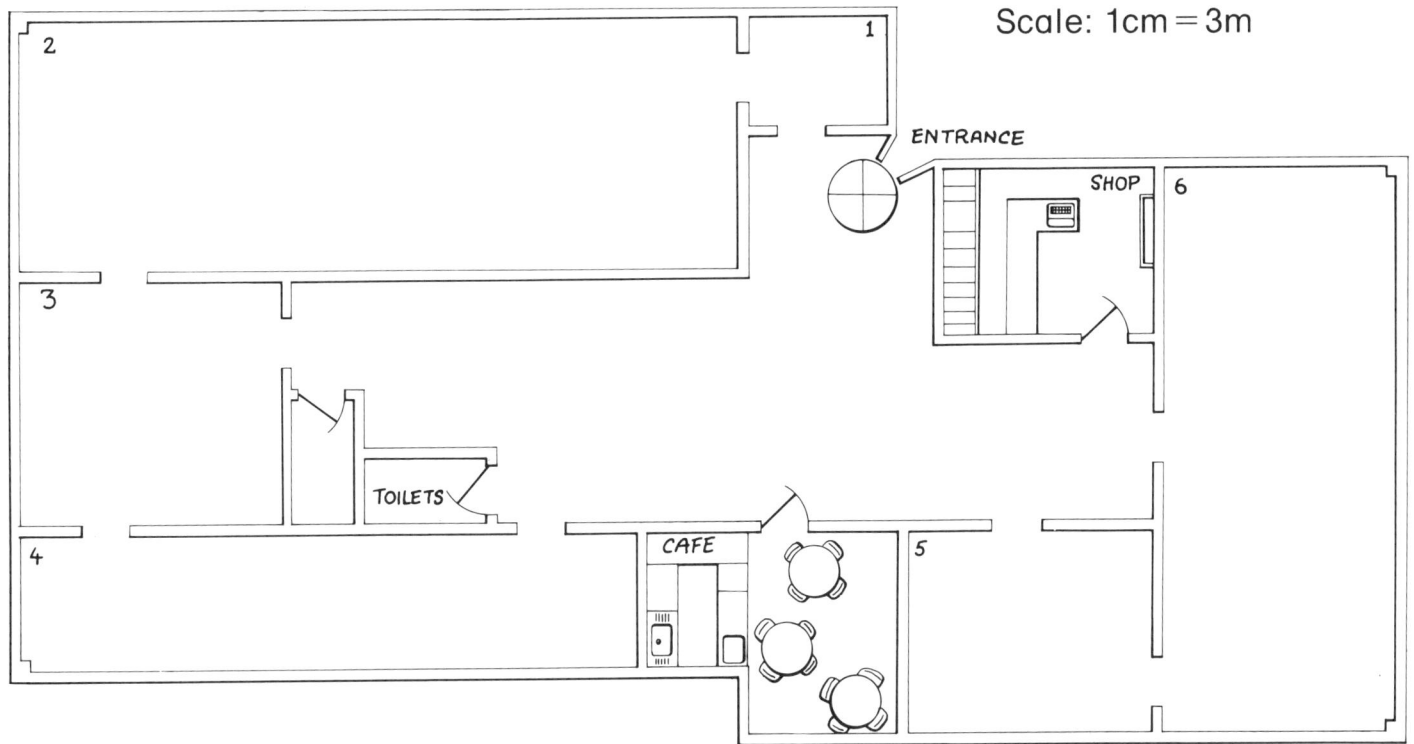

Scale: 1cm = 3m

Draw the animals in the rooms then write about what you saw in the museum.

Start like this: First I went into room 1 and I saw _____ . Then....

Why did dinosaurs become extinct? What do the scientists think?

Professor Smallbrain

Doctor Egghead

1 The carnivores ate all the herbivores. Then the carnivores had no food and they died.

2 Insects ate all the plants, so all the herbivores died. Then the carnivores had no food and they died too.

3 Small mammals ate all the dinosaurs' eggs so there were no baby dinosaurs.

4 The weather changed. It got very hot. It was too hot for the dinosaurs and they died.

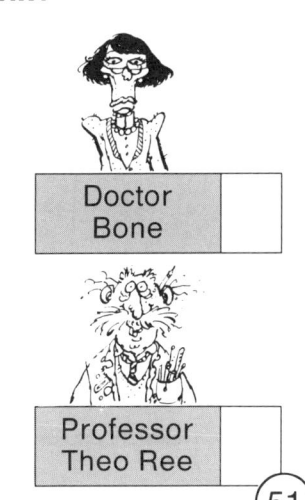

Doctor Bone

Professor Theo Ree

17

Tongue Twister

I saw a Brontosaurus.
A Brontosaurus saw me.
We saw a Stegosaurus.
A Stegosaurus saw us!

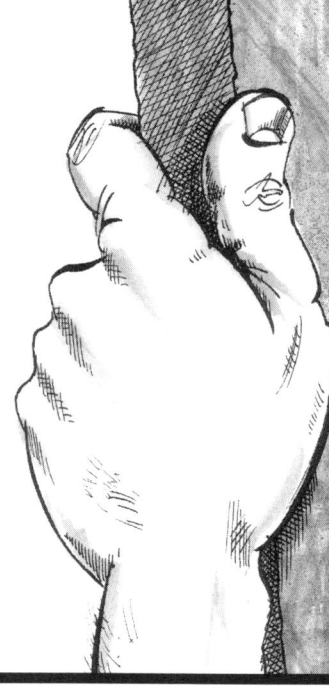

Attack! *(continued from front page)*

Mr Pen and Miss Brush worked for the Prehistoric Times: Mr Pen were a writer and Miss Brush was an artist. On Wensday they were having a piknic bai the River Dino. They were writing a story four the Times. Suddenly they saw a Tyrranasaurus. Mr Pen and Miss Brush ran away from the dinosor. The tyranosaurus chased them. They were veri lucky. Tyranisorus was too slow. It didn't catch Mr Pen and Miss Brush so it ate the piknic!

Class newspaper

1 Think of a name for your newspaper and discuss what stories you will write.
2 Write your stories.
3 Check and correct the stories.
4 Write the stories out neatly and draw pictures.
5 Cut the stories out and stick them on to the newspaper.

What other things do you find in a newspaper? Cartoons, TV guides, adverts.
Write more things to go inside your newspaper.

Nature

 **Where do they live? What's the weather like?**

Animal	Habitat	Weather
Tiger		
Crocodile		
Camel		
Polar bear		
Giraffe		

Draw the weather symbols on the map.

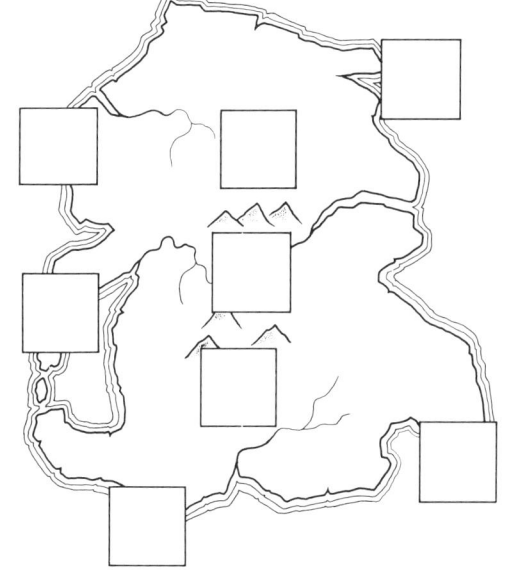

Yesterday in the north of the island it was hot and sunny. In the north-east it was sunny and cloudy for most of the day.

In the mountains it was much colder. There was some snow in the northern parts of the mountains and it rained all day in the south of the mountains.

In the south-east of the island it was cloudy and in the south-west it was cloudy and raining. In the west of the island it was hot and sunny. It was cloudy in the north-west.

Weather map

1 Draw a large map of your country.
2 Make weather symbols. Draw and colour the symbols or use coloured card.
3 What was the weather like in your country yesterday? Write a weather report.
4 Put the symbols on the map and describe the weather.

These are just a few animals in danger of extinction today.

Blue Whale
Mammal. Herbivore.
Habitat: Northern Pacific Ocean. Largest animal in the world. Up to 30m long. As long as 8 elephants. Eats small fish called plankton. No teeth. Killed for food and oil.

Giant Panda
Mammal. Omnivore.
Habitat: jungles of China. Cold region. Long black and white fur. Up to 2m long. Eats bamboo, plants and sometimes fish. Less than 1000 left in the wild. People destroying its habitat. Killed for its fur to make rugs.

Indian Rhinoceros
Mammal. Herbivore.
Habitat: Indian plain and jungle. Hot region. Thick, hard, grey skin. Up to 4m long. Eats grass and plants. Less than 700 left in the wild. Killed for its horn to make medicine. People destroying its habitat.

Mountain Gorilla
Mammal. Herbivore.
Habitat: mountains and jungles of Africa. Hot and wet region. Thick black fur. Very large. Eats fruit, flowers and plants. It is killed for sport and food. People destroying its habitat.

Nile Crocodile
Reptile. Carnivore.
Habitat: in and near African rivers. Very large. Up to 6m long. Eats birds, fish and mammals. Killed for its skin to make shoes, handbags and belts. Killed because it is dangerous and for food and medicine. People destroying its habitat.

Polar Bear
Mammal. Carnivore.
Habitat: Arctic Circle, Canada, Greenland. Very cold region. Thick white fur. Up to 3m long. Eats fish and seals. Killed for its fur and for sport. Fur used to make coats.

St Lucia Parrot
Bird. Herbivore. Habitat: St Lucia Jungle near South America. Very hot and wet region. Green, blue and orange feathers. Eats fruit. May be only 100 left in the wild. Killed for food. Collected as pets. People destroying its habitat.

Tiger
Mammal. Carnivore.
Habitat: Asian jungles. Hot and cold regions. Up to 3m long. Orange, black and white fur. Eats small mammals, fish and sometimes insects. Killed for its fur and for sport. Fur used to make coats and rugs. Killed to make medicine. People destroying its habitat.

Read the information on page 54. What animals are these?

1 They are herbivores. They live in the African jungle. They are
killed for sport.   ....

2 They are herbivores. They live on an island near South America.
They are collected as pets.   ....

3 They are carnivores. They grow up to 6m long. Their skin is
used to make handbags and shoes.   ....

4 They are mammals. They live in cold regions. There are less than
1000 left in the wild.   ....

5 They are mammals. They grow up to 30m long. They are killed
for food and oil.   ....

Giant Panda

IN DANGER

name: giant panda
group: mammal
habitat: jungle
region: China
reason: habitat, fur

The giant panda
is a large mammal.
It lives ....
....
It grows up to
..............................metres and
has ....
.... fur.

It eats ....
....
There are ....
....left in
the wild. It is in danger
because people are ....

Animal files

1 Choose an animal to write about.
Draw a picture and write notes about
the animal on the front of a file.

2 On paper write a description of the
animal and as much information as
you can.

3 Ask your friends and
your teacher to check
your work.

4 Correct the mistakes
and write it out again.

5 Put all the files made
by the class in a box in
alphabetical order.

Nature

Sponsored English Spelling Test

**A sponsored event is a way of collecting money to help a charity.
Collect money to help a wildlife organisation in your own country.**

1 Decide which organisation to collect money for.
Set a time and date for the test.
2 Make sponsor forms.
3 Ask your family and friends to sponsor you.
4 Learn to spell as many of these words as you can.

address	house
asked	laughing
beautiful	listen
because	measure
beginning	mirror
birthday	opposite
breakfast	orange
cauliflower	photograph
chair	picture
children	poisonous
chocolate	quarter
climb	restaurant
cupboard	right
dangerous	rough
difficult	said
disappointed	somewhere
eight	surprised
enormous	table
everywhere	thousand
family	tomorrow
favourite	tongue
friend	touch
ghost	vegetable
girl	women
guess	wrong

SPONSOR FORM   Name ....

Class ..... is having a sponsored English spelling test to collect money for the World Wide Fund for Nature on (date).......
There are 50 words in the test.
Please sponsor me.

Name	Address	Amount per word	Total

.... got ..... words correct in the spelling test.
Signed .... (Teacher)

5 Do the test. Then count how many words you got right.
Get your teacher to sign your form.
6 Collect the money from your family and friends.
Give it to your teacher.
Send it to the charity.

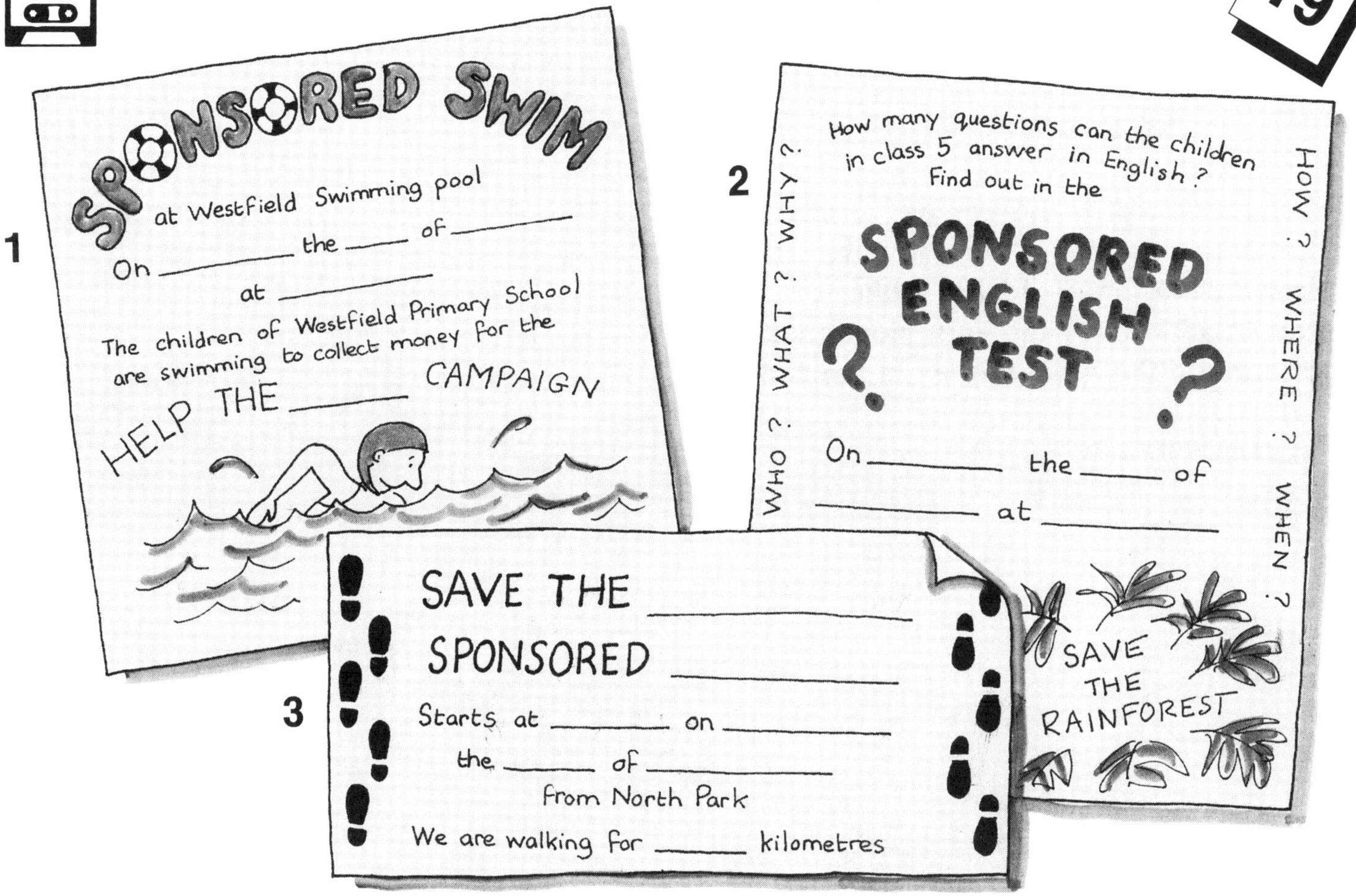
1
SPONSORED SWIM
at Westfield Swimming pool
On ________ the ____ of ________
at ________
The children of Westfield Primary School are swimming to collect money for the
HELP THE ______ CAMPAIGN
2
How many questions can the children in class 5 answer in English? Find out in the
SPONSORED ENGLISH TEST
On ________ the ______ of ________ at ________
WHO ? WHAT ? WHY ?
HOW ? WHERE ? WHEN ?
SAVE THE RAINFOREST
3
SAVE THE ________
SPONSORED ________
Starts at ______ on ________
the ______ of ________
From North Park
We are walking for _____ kilometres

Posters

Advertise your sponsored event. Or make a poster about animals in danger.

1 Make notes of the information for your poster.

What? Sponsored Spell
Who? Class 4
When? Monday 10th June at 10:00
Where? Main Hall
Why? WWF - Whales

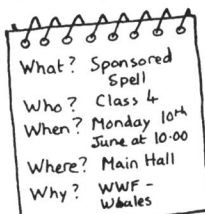

2 Try different designs for your poster.

SAVE THE WHALE
TEST
SPONSORED ENGLISH SPELLING TEST
SAVE
SAVE

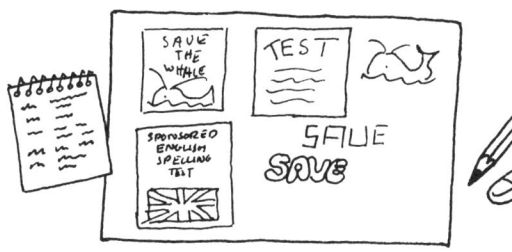

3 Choose your best design. Draw and colour a big poster.

SAVE THE WHALE
CLASS 4
WWF
SPONSORED SPELL on Monday the 10th of June at 10 o'clock in the Hall

4 Pin the poster on the wall.

NOTICES
SAVE THE WHALE

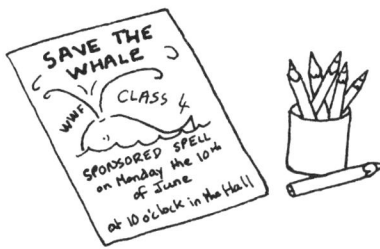

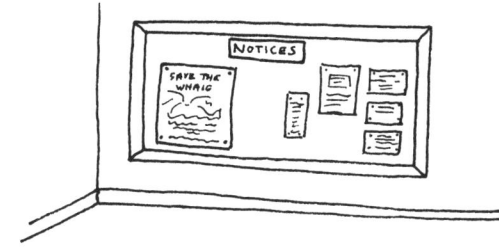

Sponsored English Spelling Test

How many words did you get right? ....

How many sponsors did you get? ....

How much money did you make? ....

How much money did your class make? ....

Who made the most money in the class? ....

Complete the letter

.... ← Name and address of school

....

....

....

.... ← Date

Dear Sir,

Our class had a competition to collect money to save animals in danger. There are .... children in our class. We collected .... by learning to spell words in English. My own language is .... We did this in our English lesson.

Please use this money to help save .... or any other animals

Yours sincerely,

Signatures of class

WWF
Panda House
Godalming
Surrey
GU7 1XR
England

PAR AVION
BY AIR MAIL

Nature

Use these cards with the game on page 40 of your Coursebook.

animal:	animal:	animal:	animal:
food:	food:	food:	food:
habitat:	habitat:	habitat:	habitat:
saved from:	saved from:	saved from:	saved from:

animal:	animal:	animal:	animal:
food:	food:	food:	food:
habitat:	habitat:	habitat:	habitat:
saved from:	saved from:	saved from:	saved from:

 **Tongue Twister**

Sid saw Sammy steal the
sabre-toothed tiger's teeth.

How many words can you make in five minutes from the letters in this dinosaur? What is the dinosaur's name?

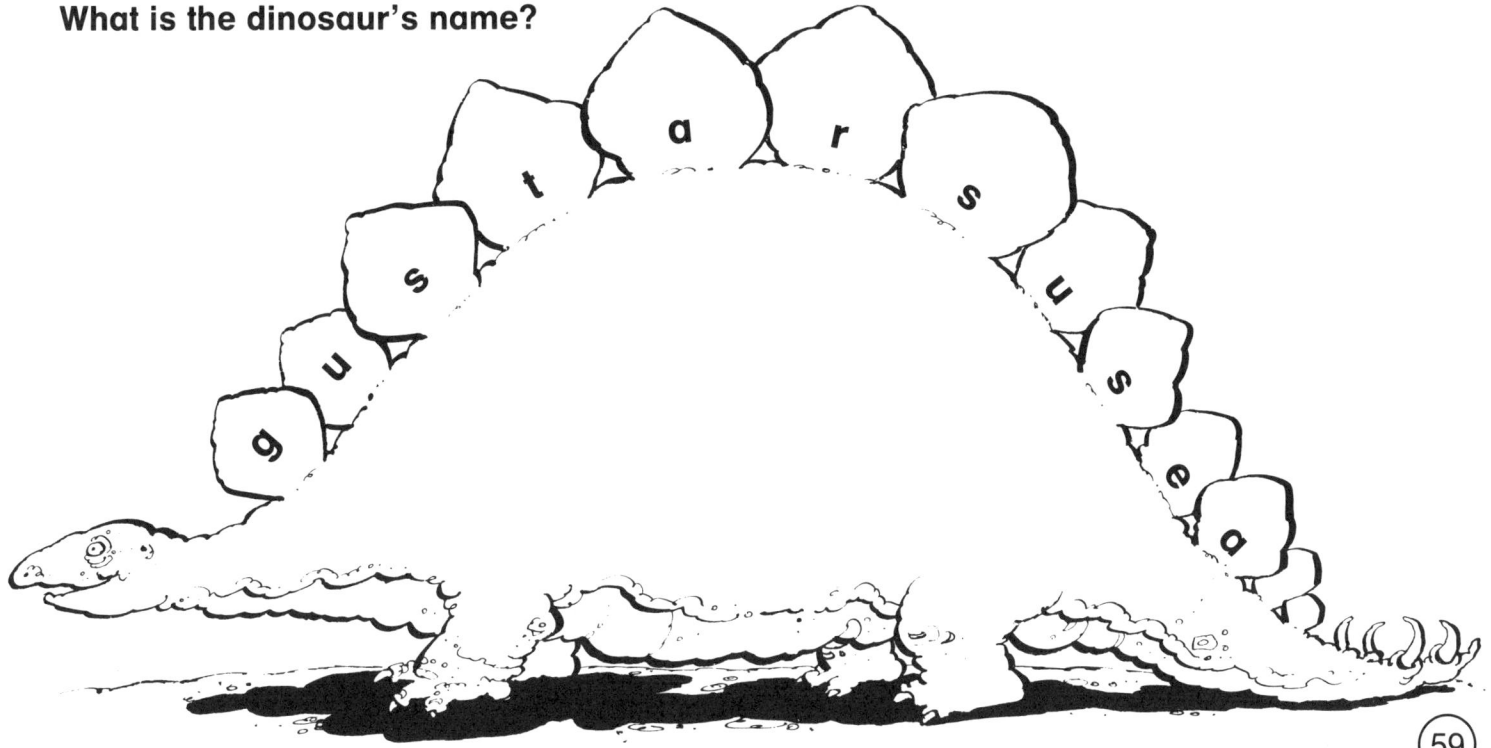

What animals have you got in your country? Do you know what kind of animals they are? Are any of them in danger of becoming extinct?

Species	Group	In danger?

Look at pages 10-11 in your Reader. Answer these questions.

1 What kind of animals have gills?
2 How many different kinds of reptile are there?
3 Are amphibians warm-blooded?
4 Do fish lay eggs?
5 Most reptiles have scales. What other animals have scales?
6 When did dinosaurs become extinct?
7 How much did Brachiosaurus weigh?
8 What was the name of the fastest dinosaur?
9 Was Pteranodon a bird?
10 How long was Diplodocus?

Look at the notes and read the description.

- cheetah
- mammal
- carnivore - eats large and small mammals
- habitat - plains of Africa - hot region
- large cat - up to 2m long
- yellow/orange fur with black spots
- fastest land animal
- killed for its fur - to make coats and rugs

The cheetah is a mammal. It is a carnivore and it eats large and small mammals. It lives on the African plains. It is a large cat. It grows up to two metres long and has yellow/orange fur with black spots.

It is the fastest land animal in the world. It is now in danger of becoming extinct because it is killed for its fur. Its fur is used to make coats and rugs.

Now read these notes and write a description of this animal.

- African elephant
- mammal
- herbivore - eats grass and plants
- habitat - plains of Africa - hot region
- largest land animal - up to 3.5m high
- thick, rough, grey skin
- killed for its ivory tusks to make ornaments

Space

What film is this robot in? What is its name?
Do you know any other space films?
Do you know any TV programmes about space?
Do you know any books about space?
Do you know any space stories in comics?

In your exercise book write a list of all the space stories you know and the names of the characters. Which one is your favourite?

Make a Planet Mobile

You need:
large sheets of card · ruler · pencil · scissors · coloured pencils · needle and cotton · 1m cane

Scale sizes	
planets	radius
Mercury	0.5cm
Venus	1.3cm
Earth	1.3cm
Mars	0.68cm
Jupiter	14.3cm
Saturn	12cm
Uranus	5cm
Neptune	48cm
Pluto	0.6cm

Make the planets.

1 Work in groups of four. Decide which planets each person will make.

2 Draw the circles. E.g. for Uranus measure points in a circle 5cm from the centre. Then connect the points to make a circle.

3 Cut out the circle.

4 To make the ring first draw around the circle. Then draw a circle inside and outside the first circle. Cut out the ring.

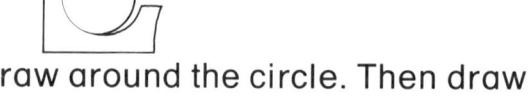

5 Colour the planet and the ring.

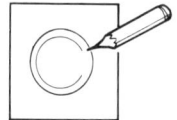

6 Make two small cuts in the planet. Push the planet inside the ring.

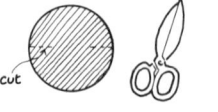

7 Fix a piece of cotton to the top of each planet. Use a needle.

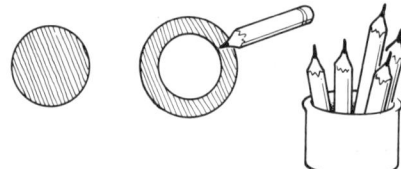
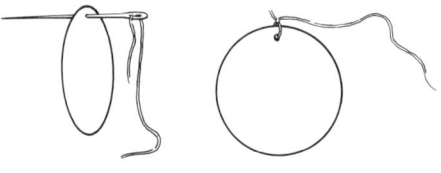

8 Tie each planet to the cane.

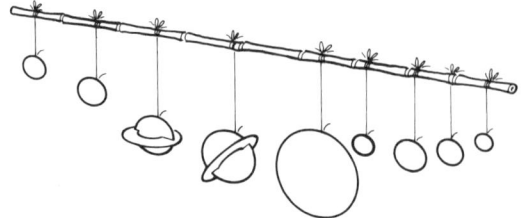

 **What do you know about space? Connect the questions and answers.**

1 When did the first rocket go into space?

2 When did the first man go into space?

3 What was the name of the first rocket to go into space?

4 What was the first rocket to land on Mars?

5 Who was the first man to go into space?

6 Who was the first man on the moon?

7 What was the name of the first space station?

8 Who was the first woman in space?

9 When did the first men land on the moon?

10 When did the dog Laika go into space?

A Salyut 1

B Neil Armstrong

C Yuri Gagarin

D Valentina Tereshkova

E 4 October 1957

F Sputnik 1

G Viking 1

H 12 April 1961

I 20 July 1969

J 3 November 1957

The Balloon Rocket Race

You need:  a balloon 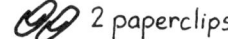 2 paperclips  tape  string

1 Make the rocket

Work in groups of four. Think of a name for your rocket.
Bend the paper clips like this: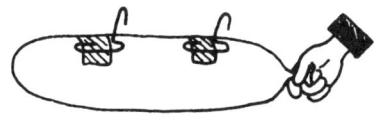
Blow up the balloon and hold the end.
Stick the paper clips onto the balloon with tape.
Let the air out of the balloon slowly.

2 The race

Fix one end of the string to a chair and the other end to the wall.
Choose one person from your group to release the rocket.
Blow up the balloon. Hold the end.
Put the balloon rocket onto the string
Then let it go.
How far did your rocket go?
Measure the distance.

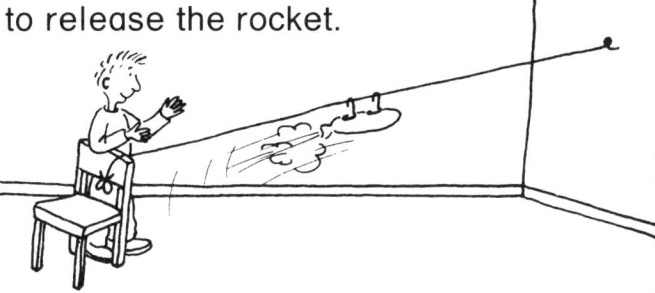

How far did each rocket go? Which rocket went the furthest? Who won the race?

Label the planets.

Fact File .... planets

planet	approximate distance from sun (million km)	approximate diameter (km)	time taken to orbit sun (years + days)
Mercury	58		
Venus		12,300	
Earth		12,756	
Mars			1 year 321 days
Jupiter	778		
Saturn		120,000	
Uranus			84 years 6 days
Neptune		48,400	
Pluto	5907		

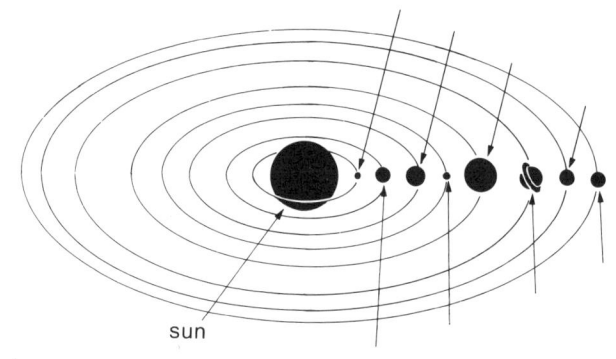

sun

This is our ....
Our planet is called ....
There is one .... and nine ....
in our solar system.
Our solar system is in the ....
.... galaxy.

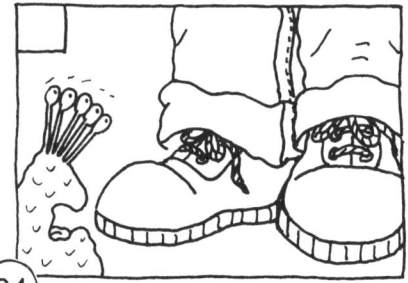

Listen to Professor Prediction talking about robots. What can robots do now? What will they do in the future?

| speak | wash up | sweep the floor | dance | play tennis | draw | read | ride a bike |

< FUTURE >

My robot

How would Washy the Robot answer these questions?

Can you play the piano?
No, ...

Do you like washing clothes?
Yes, ...

Are you good at drawing?
No, ...

Are you a clever robot?
Yes, ...

Which way?

← left	→ right	↑ up	↓ down	stop

These are talking robots. They speak English. But each robot has a problem.
They keep making mistakes. They always make the same kind of mistake.
Find the mistakes and correct them.

1 I is going to the shops.

....

Yesterday she goed to the cinema.

....

The giraffe have got a long neck.

....

There are your pen. It are on the table.

....

Do you play football yesterday?

....

2 I want a hat small please.

....

English is difficult very.

....

She had black long hair.

....

The blue whale is the larger animal in the world.

....

3 Do you want a orange or a apple?

....

I went to the Italy last year.

....

The Maria is five years old.

....

An elephant is very big animal.

....

Space

Look at pages 46 and 47 of your Coursebook.

1 How do you write Monza's name in Martian? ....

2 What is this word in English? ⇔ ◎ ◎ ✪ ....

3 Is ≋ before or after ✳ in the Martian alphabet? ....

4 What is Monza's comic called? What is it about? ....

5 Is ▤ before or after ⚠ in the Martian alphabet? ....

This is the electroboard from Monza's classroom. What does it say? Can you help Monza?

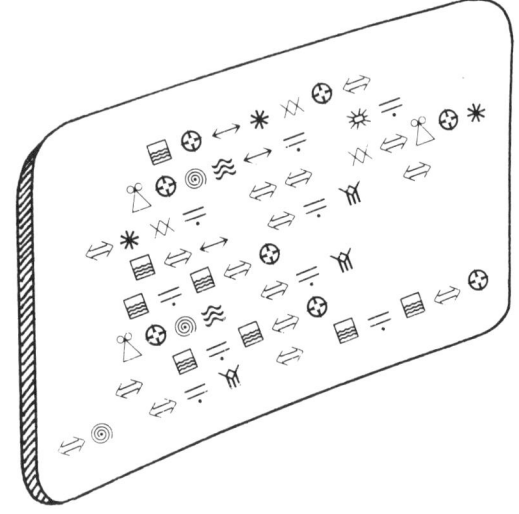

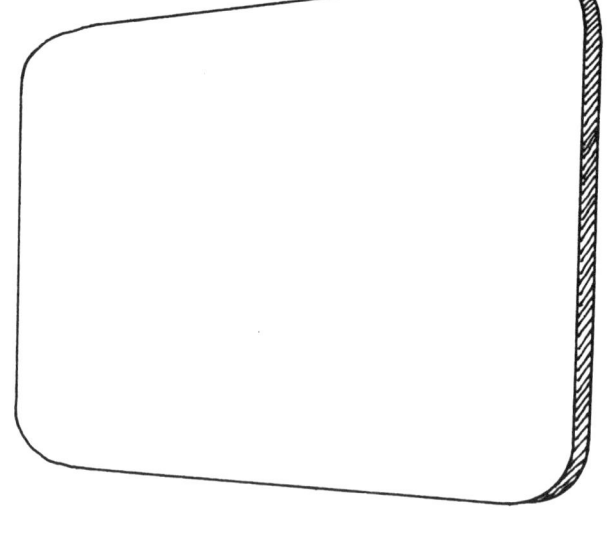

Write these words in alphabetical order.

....
....
....
....
....
....
....
....
....

Monza's spaceship is going to Earth. The passengers come from all over the galaxy. What do the other passengers look like?

There are some very strange creatures sitting next to Monza.

23

Monza is on Earth now. He is standing outside your school. He is carrying his suitcase and a list. All travellers with Earth Holidays get a list. But Monza doesn't understand his list because he isn't very good at English. Can you help him?

EARTH HOLIDAYS PLC

GUIDE TO LEARNING ENGLISH

1. Find a school and some Earth children to help you.
2. Are there any English words that are the same as or similar to words in your own language? What are they?
3. Ask your Earth friends to teach you the most important words and questions in English.
4. Try some of these ideas:
   Read English books and comics
   Watch English TV programmes
   Listen to English music
   Learn some English songs
   Go to English lessons
   Do your homework
5. Get a book to help you with your English.

Look at these Martian words. What do they mean? Do you know how to pronounce them? Listen to the tape. Do they sound like words in your language? Which words do they sound like? Do they mean the same?

Martian words	English meaning	Sounds like . . .	Does it sound like a word in your language?	Does it mean the same?
↔ ⊕ ✳ ≋ ⚊	taxi			
✳ ⊕ ✳ ⊕	mother			
◎ ⇔	no			
✳ ⊕ ✳ ⚊	bad			
✳ ⇔ ✳ ⊕	how			

How many English words sound like words in your language? Make a list.

Putting on a Play

1 Choose the **actors** and **actresses**.
 (These are the people who will be in the play.)
2 Choose a **director**.
 (This is the person who helps the actors by telling
 them what to do, how to speak, when to move.)
3 Read the play from start to finish.
4 Next, think about the **characters** in the play.
 – What do they look like?
 – How do they walk or move?
 – How do they speak?
5 Read the play again.
 Remember – How does your character speak?

6 Learn your **lines**.
 (That means the words you will speak in the play.)
 – Get a friend to help you.
 – Write your lines onto pieces of paper.
 – Practice in the bath!
 – If you can't remember your lines, use **cue cards**.
 (Write the lines on paper and read them.)

7 Make **masks** and **costumes** (see Activity Book page 72.)
8 Make **programmes** for the play (see Activity Book page 73.)
9 Then practise the play on **stage**.
 – Where will you stand?
 – Where will you move to?
 – How quickly will you move?
10 Divide the play into smaller parts. Practise
 each part separately on the stage.

11 Practise all the parts together wearing your
 masks and costumes. Remember these things.
 – How the characters speak.
 – How the characters move.
 – Where the characters move.
12 Then you will be ready to put on your play
 for the whole school.

Masks

You need: scissors glue a pencil coloured pencils

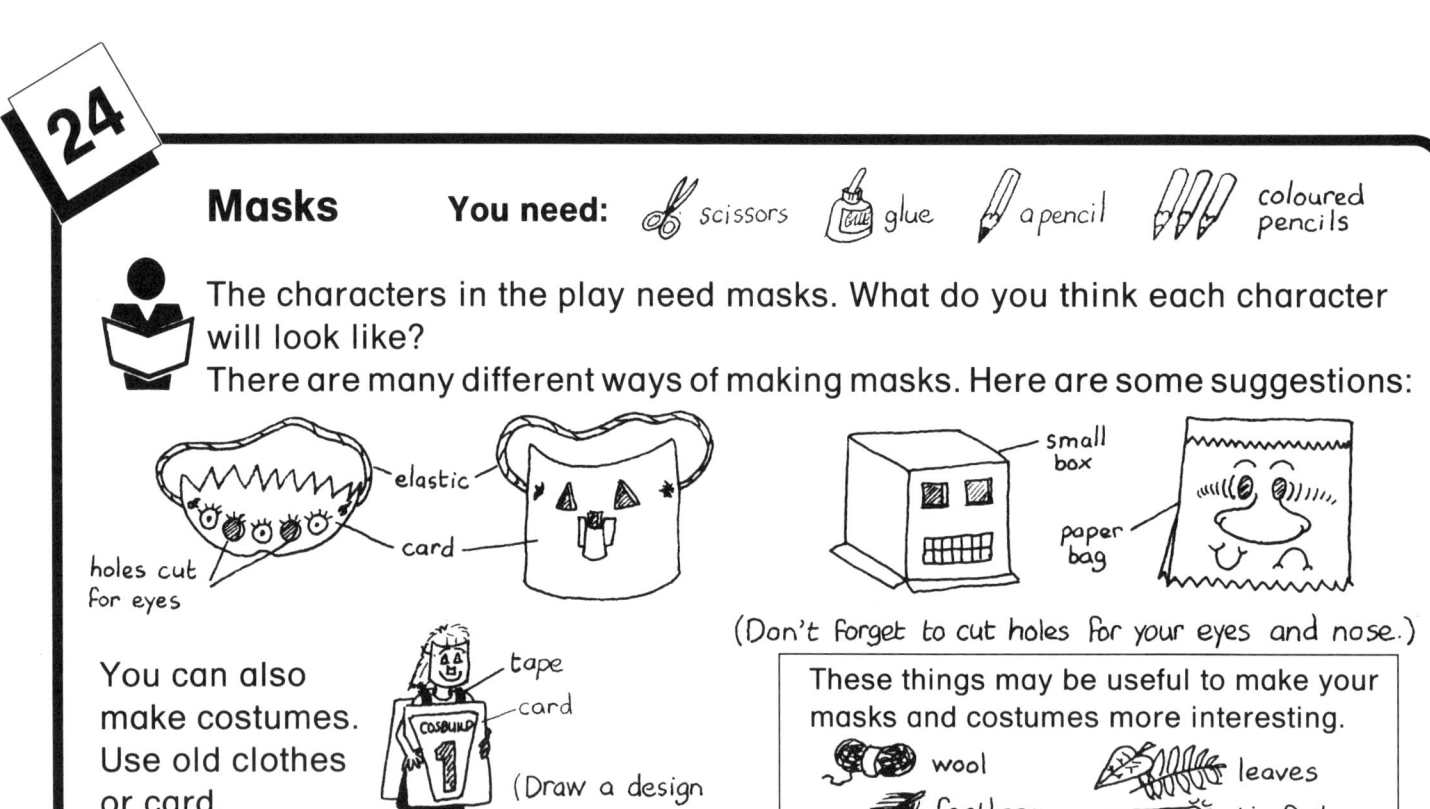

The characters in the play need masks. What do you think each character will look like?

There are many different ways of making masks. Here are some suggestions:

elastic

card

holes cut for eyes

small box

paper bag

(Don't forget to cut holes for your eyes and nose.)

You can also make costumes. Use old clothes or card.

tape

card

(Draw a design or stick things onto the card.)

These things may be useful to make your masks and costumes more interesting.

wool   leaves

feathers   tin foil

coloured card

How do Captain Clanger and the crew of COSBUILD 1 escape from Echo Galaxy?

There are many other ways to escape from the Galaxy.

One way is to speak more quickly than the Echo.

Can you think of any more ways?

Put these lines in the correct order. Who says each line?

- [ ] .... How did you know?
- [ ] .... Me too. Beep.
- [ ] .... Well, I can't see anything else.
- [ ] .... Spaceship.
- [ ] .... I know.
- [ ] .... We're bored. Who wants to play I-spy?
- [ ] .... We'll go first.
- [ ] .... Me.
- [ ] .... The Captain always goes first.
- [ ] .... No. I'll go first. I'm the Captain.
- [ ] .... Because it's always 'spaceship'. You play every day. And it's always 'spaceship'.
- [ ] .... I spy with one of my eyes something beginning with S.

Now check your answers in your Reader.

Can you remember the lines in the play?

CAPTAIN	....
ECHO	now now now now now now
ORK-ORK	....
ECHO	that that that that that that
CAPTAIN	....
ECHO	happening happening happening happening happening happening
ICU2	....
ECHO	galaxy galaxy galaxy galaxy galaxy galaxy
ICU2	....
ECHO	echoed echoed echoed echoed echoed echoed
ORK-ORK	....
ECHO	stupid stupid stupid stupid stupid stupid
ZUBS	....
ECHO	zub zub zub zub zub zub
BEEP	....
ECHO	beep beep beep beep beep beep
ICU2	....
ECHO	go go go go go go
RON-NANCY	....
ECHO	easy easy easy easy easy easy
EVERYBODY	....
ECHO	go go go go go go
CAPTAIN	....
ECHO	happening happening happening happening happening happening

Now check your answers in your Reader.

Programmes

You need:  paper a pen a pencil coloured pencils

1 Fold the paper.

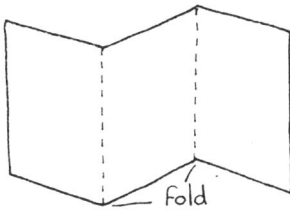

2 On the first page write the name, the date and the time of the play.

3 On the second page write an introduction to the play.

4 On the third page write the names of the characters and the actors.

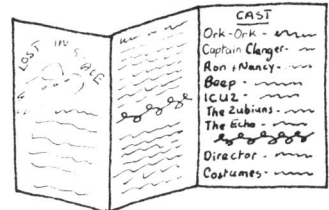

Space

Work in groups of four.
Talk about life in the future.

	Names			
Do you think people will live on other planets?				
Do you think people will have holidays in space?				
Do you think everyone will have a robot?				
Do you think everyone will use a computer?				
Do you think **you** will travel in space?				

What does your class think about life in the future? Look at each question.

% % Percentages % %

How many people said 'yes'?   A ☐

How many people are there in your class?   B ☐

Divide A by B and multiply by 100 (use a calculator)

A ÷ B × 100 = ... %

Write sentences in your exercise book.

...... % of people think that people will live on other planets.

...... % of people think that people won't live on other planets.

Life in the future

 **Space Code** **Listen. Put a ✗ in the squares.**

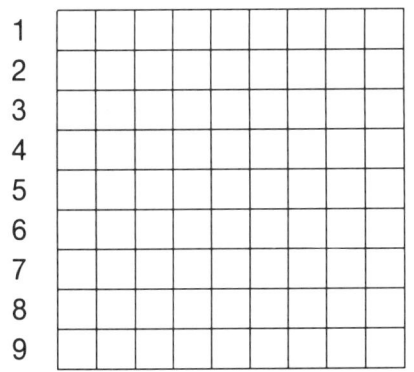

Listen for the sound /sh/
(in the word *sheep*)

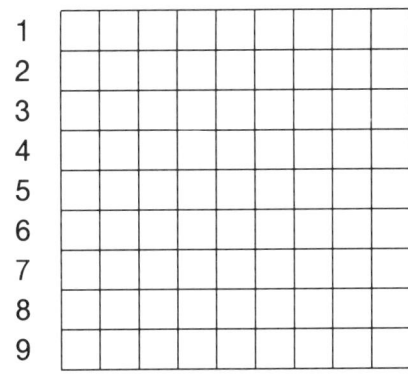

Listen for the sound /ee/
(in the word *meat*)

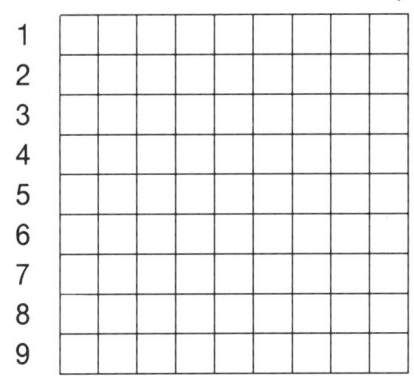

Listen for the sound /b/
(in the word *big*)

Tongue Twister

When will Riley write to Wally?
Wally wants to know.

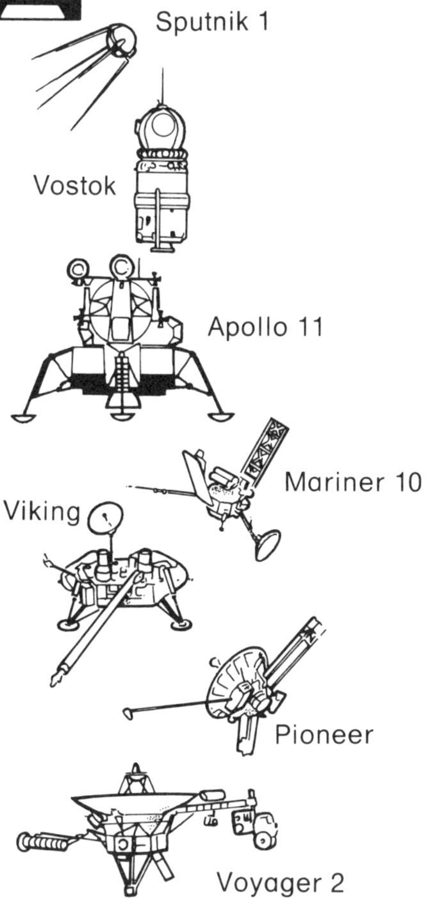

Sputnik 1

Vostok

Apollo 11

Mariner 10

Viking

Pioneer

Voyager 2

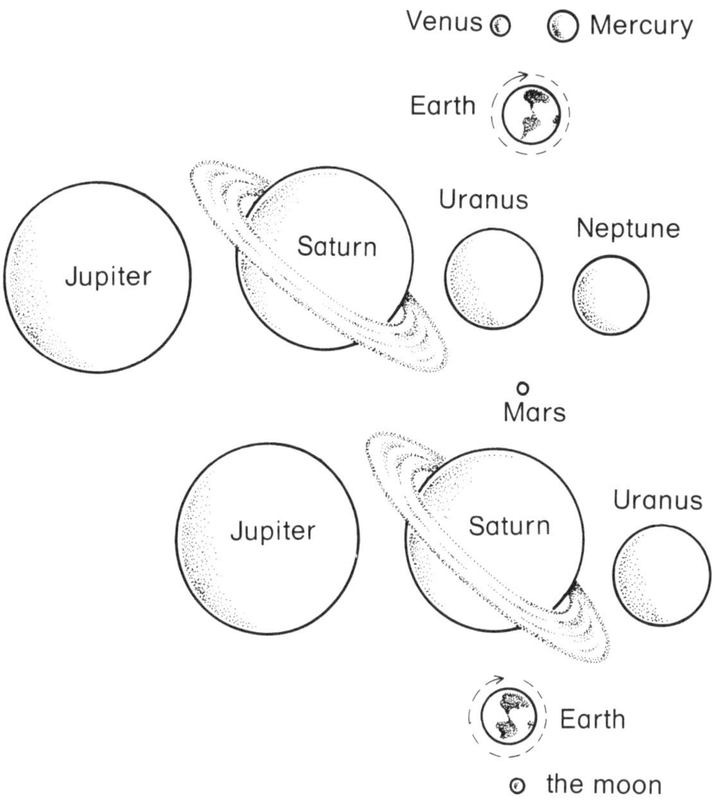

Venus   Mercury

Earth

Uranus

Saturn   Neptune

Jupiter

Mars

Jupiter   Saturn   Uranus

Earth

the moon

Put these sentences in the correct order.

□ The spaceship landed quite near Sally.

□ Suddenly she heard a loud noise.

□ Sally was walking to school.

□ and it had . . .

□ Sally was very scared.

□ It was about two metres tall

□ She looked up and saw a spaceship.

□ There was a strange alien creature inside the ship.

□ She was late again.

□ Then the door of the spaceship opened.

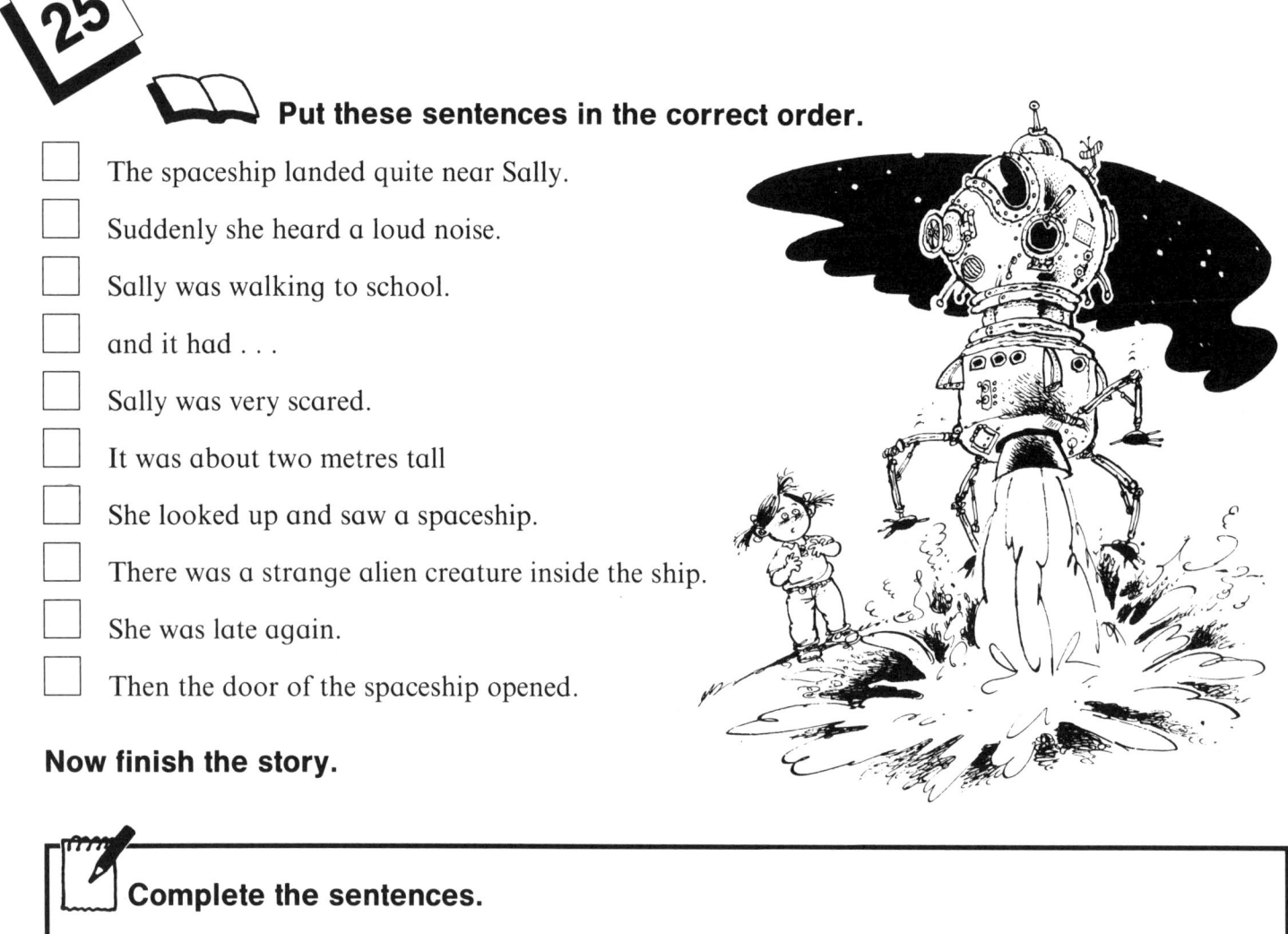

Now finish the story.

Complete the sentences.

| was / largest / will / were / did / nearest / will / are / is / Do |

1 Mercury is the .... planet to the sun.

2 .... you like films about space?

3 Who .... the first men on the moon?

4 Jupiter .... between Saturn and Mars.

5 When .... Neil Armstrong go to the moon?

6 Jupiter is the .... planet in our solar system.

7 In the future people .... travel in space.

8 Yuri Gagarin .... the first man in space.

9 Tomorrow we .... go to school.

10 There .... nine planets in our solar system.

My Story

1 What is Supersnake writing? ....

2 Where does Supersnake come from? ....

3 When did he say his first word? ....

4 What was his first word? ....

5 What was his favourite subject at school? ....

6 How many sisters has he got? ....

7 Why can't Supersnake go home? ....

8 What is Ratman's real name? ....

9 What is Ratman's car called? ....

10 What is Supersnake going to do next? ....

dad's hat

s
t
r
o
n
g

Down

● The planet Viper is in the Serpiente _____ . (6)

● Supersnake says he is _____ . (6)

● Supersnake landed on _____ . (5)

● _____ escaped in his Ratmobile. (6)

● Supersnake got his first _____ when he was five weeks old. (5)

● Supersnake was the cleverest _____ in his class. (5)

Across

● Supersnake's fish was called _____ . (4)

● Supersnake _____ a record. (4)

● Supersnake's favourite toy was a big blue _____ . (6)

● Supersnake got _____ in space. (4)

● Supersnake was sitting in the cafe eating an ____ . (3)

● Supersnake wanted to be an _____ . (9)

● Supersnake wanted to be a fireman. He used to wear his dad's _____ . (3)

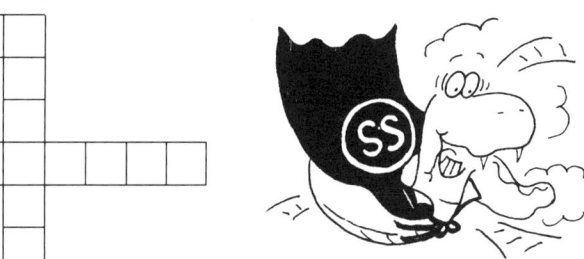

PERSONAL FACTS

Surname ....

First name(s) ....

Address ....

....

Country ....

Telephone number ....

Nationality ....

Date of birth ....

APPEARANCE

Height ....

Weight ....

Colour of eyes ....

Colour of hair ....

Shoe size ....

FAMILY

Number of people in family ....

Brother(s) – name(s) ....

           age(s) ....

Sister(s) – name(s) ....

           age(s) ....

Pet(s) ....

HOME

House or flat ....

Garden/balcony ....

Number of rooms ....

Car ....

SCHOOL

Name of school ....

Address ....

....

Class ....

Teacher ....

Number of pupils: boys .... girls ....

SPORTS AND HOBBIES

Main hobbies ....

....

Other hobbies ....

....

Sports I watch ....

....

Sports I play ....

....

ROUTINE

Time I get up: weekdays ....

          weekend ....

Time I go to bed: weekdays ....

          weekend ....

Time I go to school ....

Autobiography

Think of a title and design a cover for your book.

You could:
draw pictures   or stick a photo   or write words.

Think about things you like – food, pop stars, TV, hobbies, sports etc.

Ask your family

When was I born?
What time was I born?
Where was I born?
How much did I weigh?
When did I start to crawl?
When did I start to walk?
When did I get my first tooth?
When did I say my first word?
What was my first word?

BABY FACTS

Name ....
Date of birth ....
Time of birth ....
Born at ....
Weight ....
Started to crawl ....
Started to walk ....
First tooth ....
Said the first word ....
First word was ....

got	was	started	was	got	said	had

Supersnake .... born on the planet Viper. He weighed 18 grammes. He was eight centimetres long. He .... his first tooth when he was five weeks old. He .... his first word at nine months. His favourite toy .... a big blue rattle. He .... a pet fish called Sink. He .... his first bike when he was two years old and he .... school when he was four.

Autobiography

Write about your early life.

Write about when and where you were born, your first tooth, your first word etc. What else can you remember?

A favourite toy   A special event   Special people   A bad event   First day at school

Fred bear

Happy Birthday

My best Friend

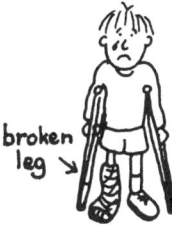

broken leg

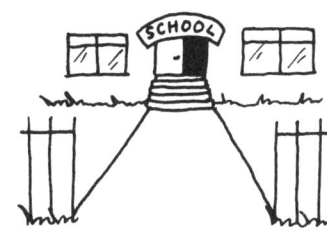

SCHOOL

79

My Story

THE Vampire Family Tree

Vera

 ## Write the names

 My name is Vera Vampire. This is my family tree. I've got an older brother and a younger sister. My brother's name is Vince and my sister's name is Viola. My mother's name is Val and my father's name is Viv. My aunt is called Verity and my uncle is called Vic.

I've got two cousins. Virginia is older than me and her brother Virgil is younger than me. My grandmother and grandfather's names are Valeria and Victor Vampire. My great grandmother's name is Vine Vampire and my great grandfather's name is Vernon Vampire.

	Write the names here
Who's got the most cousins?	
Find four people who have got two sisters.	
Find one person who is the oldest child in their family.	
Find someone who hasn't got any sisters.	
Find two boys who have got one older sister.	
Who's got the biggest family in your class?	
Who's got a sister whose name begins with **A**?	
Who's got a brother whose name begins with **S**?	

Autobiography

Write about your family.

Have you got any brothers, sisters or cousins? Are they older or younger than you? Who is the oldest in your family? Who is the youngest? Have you got aunts and uncles? Do they live in the same town as you?

Draw your family tree.
Write the names and ages.

OR

Make a chart about your family.
List the names, ages and relationships.

The Smith Family Tree

Edna Smith 72   Harry Smith -73

Mary Green

My Family			
Names	Ages	He/She is my....	I am his/her....
Bill Weston	57	grandfather	grandaughter
Ann Weston	14	oldest sister	younger sister

 **Where do they sit?**

There must be boys only on the front row.
Monsters and Vampires must not sit at the back.
Monsters must not sit next to Vampires.
Boys must not sit next to girls.
Horace Horror must sit next to the door.
Bert Blood must sit as far away as possible from Mick Monster.
Neil Nasty must sit on the front row.

Frank Stein must not sit at the front.
Neil Nasty must not sit next to Horace Horror.
Frank Stein must not sit near the window.
Wilma Witch must sit next to the window.
Norma Nasty must sit on the back row.
Edna Evil must sit next to the window.
Sisters must not sit behind brothers.

window

Boys
Vince Vampire
Frank Stein
Neil Nasty
Bert Blood
Mick Monster
Horace Horror

Girls
Vera Vampire
Wendy Wolf
Norma Nasty
Edna Evil
Mandy Monster
Wilma Witch

door

front row →

back row →

School Facts

Name of school .... Teacher's name ....

Address .... Class ....

.... Best subject ....

Worst subject ....

Number of pupils .... Things you like doing ....

Number of teachers ....

Number of classrooms .... Things you don't like doing ....

Number of classes ....

Autobiography

Draw a plan of your classroom.

Use a large piece of paper.
Label the objects.
Ask everyone in the class to sign your plan.

PLAN OF CLASSROOM 5 – CLASS B4

BIN – O
BLACKBOARD
Mrs Benson
TEACHER'S DESK
DOOR
WINDOW
Maria Brown | John Clark
Sarah Allen | Ann Shaw

Autobiography

Write about a special event.

Illustrate your story.
Use photographs, drawings, tickets or pictures from magazines.

The Wedding

My aunt Anne

On Friday the 10th of June I went to my aunt Anne's wedding. It was a sunny day. Anne's

---

Autobiography

Other things to write about in your autobiography.

Where you live OR **Household jobs** OR **Describe someone in your family or your best friend**

Describe your house. | Who washes up? | What do they look like?
Describe your room. | Who cleans the car? | What do they like doing?
Draw pictures and plans. | Make a chart like this: | What are their hobbies?

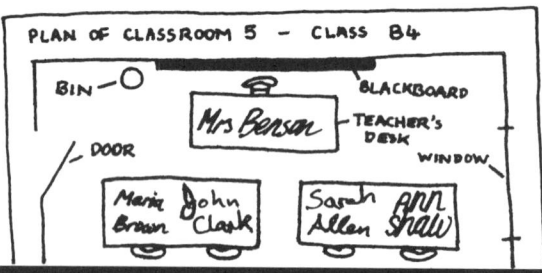

My House
Address : 52 Marsh Road, Leeds, Yorkshire England.
My house has got fire rooms. The living room is ll

Household Jobs

Names	Jobs
Me	wash up (sometimes) tidy my room
Mum	wash up, shopping, wash clothes, clean

My Best Friend

My best friend is called Anne. She is eleven years old. She's got

My Story

Autobiography

Write about things you like and don't like.

What are you afraid of?
What can you do?
What can't you do?
What are your hobbies?
Are you good at sport?

Illustrate your writing with drawings, photos or pictures from magazines.

Things I like and don't like

SPORTS
✓   ✗

In my spare time I like playing football. I'm very good at football. I don't like playing tennis or basketball.

FEARS
✓   ✗

I'm afraid of lots of things. I'm afraid of spiders and

	Write the names here
Find three people who like bananas.	
Find a boy who is afraid of spiders.	
Find someone who doesn't like cheese.	
Find two people who like playing basketball.	
Find someone whose favourite food is hamburgers.	
Find a girl who is afraid of mice.	
Find someone who collects stamps.	
Find someone whose favourite animal is a tiger.	

Autobiography

Write about your favourite things.

Think about:

food	hobbies	days
drinks	TV programmes	months
fruit	school subjects	people
vegetables	pop stars	sports
colours	films	comics

Can you think of anything else?

Illustrate your work with drawings, photographs or pictures from magazines.

☆ My Favourites ☆

My favourite food is chips
My favourite pop star is Michael Jackson
My favourite television

28

? Can you remember when you were five years old? What did you look like? What was your favourite toy? Was your hair longer or shorter than it is now? What kind of food did you like? Are you different now? What were your parents and grandparents like when they were eleven? Were they the same as you? Were they different? How different was their life?

Answer these questions.
Then ask an adult in your family the same questions.

	Me	My ....
1 Do/Did you have a pet?		
2 Does/Did your family have a car?		
3 Are/Were there computers in your school?		
4 Does/Did your family have a television?		
5 Does/Did your family have a stereo?		
6 Do/Did you have a bike?		
7 Does/Did your family have a telephone?		
8 Do/Did you live in a house or a flat?		
9 Does/Did your family have a video?		
10 Do/Did you speak another language?		
11 Are/Were there more than thirty children in your class?		
12 How many children are/were there in your family?		
13 How old were you when you started school?		

(I am .... **years old now. My** .... **was** .... **in** .... **.)**

Autobiography

Now write some sentences about your questionnaire.
Is life different today?

<u>Me and My Grandmother</u>

My life today is very different from my grandmother's life when she was eleven.
We have a video but my grandmother didn't have a video.
I have a bike and my grandmother had a bike too.

Class Surveys

Choose *one* of the questions below.
Ask everyone in the class the question. Write down their answers.
You will need to make a chart:

Names \ Colours	blue	brown	green	grey
Anne Jones		✓		
Tom Smith	✓			
Marie Hall		✓		

What colour are your eyes?

OR

What colour are your eyes?

Names	Colours
Anne Jones	brown
Tom Smith	blue
Marie Hall	brown

1 Have you got a pet? If yes, what is it?

2 How many brothers and sisters have you got?

3 What is your favourite colour?

4 What colour are your eyes?

5 What is your favourite food?

6 Do you live in a house or a flat?

7 How many rooms are there in your house?

8 Can you play the piano?

9 Do you collect things? If yes, what do you collect?

10 What time do you usually get up?

11 Do you like learning English?

Make a graph to show your results.

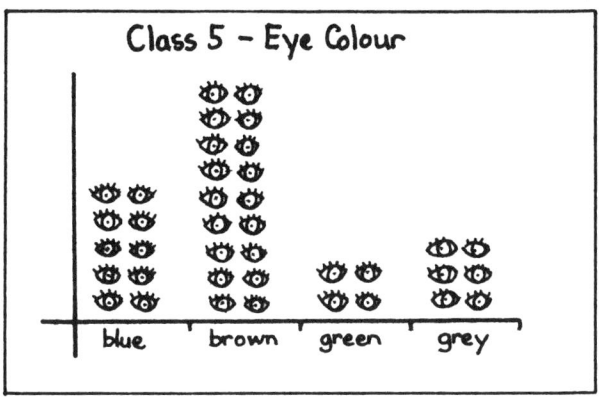

Class 5 – Eye Colour

OR

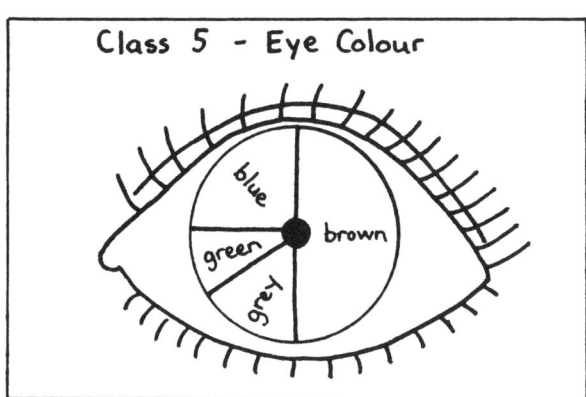

Class 5 – Eye Colour

My Story

Make a Fortune Teller

You need: 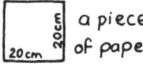 a piece of paper  a pen

1 Fold the paper in half.

 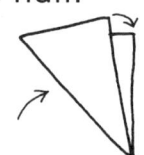

2 Fold the paper in half again.

3 Unfold the paper.

middle — corner

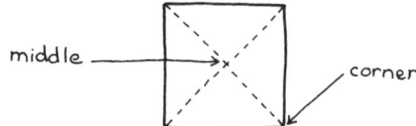

4 Fold each corner into the middle.

 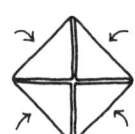

5 Write a colour on each triangle.

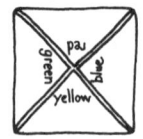 

6 Turn the square over.

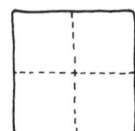

7 Fold each corner into the middle again.

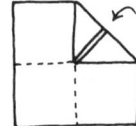 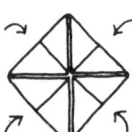

8 Write a number between 1 and 30 on each of the eight triangles.

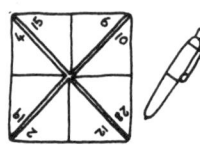

9 Fold the square in half twice.

first 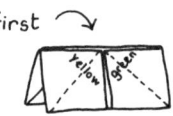 second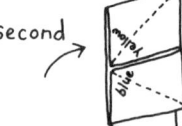

10 Unfold. Then lift the flaps. Write a 'fortune' in each triangle.

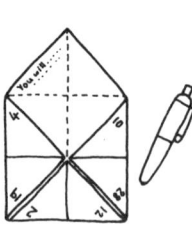 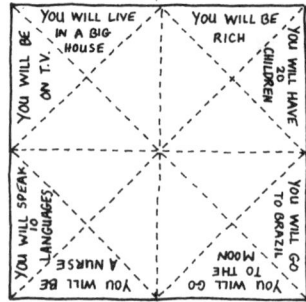

11 Fold the flaps down again.

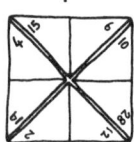

12 Put your thumb and first finger into the flaps.

How to use your Fortune Teller

Work with a friend. Move your Fortune Teller as you spell and count.

A Pick a colour.
B Red.
A R-E-D.
A Pick a number.
B Four.
A 1-2-3-4.
A Pick a number.
B Ten.
A (Open the flap.) You will be rich!

Autobiography

Write about your future.

What do you think will happen?
Will you get married?
Will you have children?
Will you have a car?
Where will you live?

Illustrate your story.

My Future

When I grow up I will be famous. I will live in a big house by the sea. I will

 Listen to the tape. Who is working?

secretary

teacher

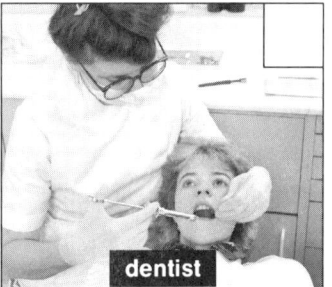

dentist

shop assistant

fireman

doctor

sports woman

police officer

Game: What's my job?

Do you work inside?
Do you work outside?
Do you work with children?
Do you work with your hands?
Do you work with other people?
Do you wear a hat?
Do you play a sport?
Is your job dangerous?
Do you sell things?
Do you help people?

Autobiography

What do you want to do when you grow up?

Draw a picture and write about what you want to be.

Jobs

When I grow up I want to be a doctor. I want to work in a big hospital. I want to

SUPERSNAKE

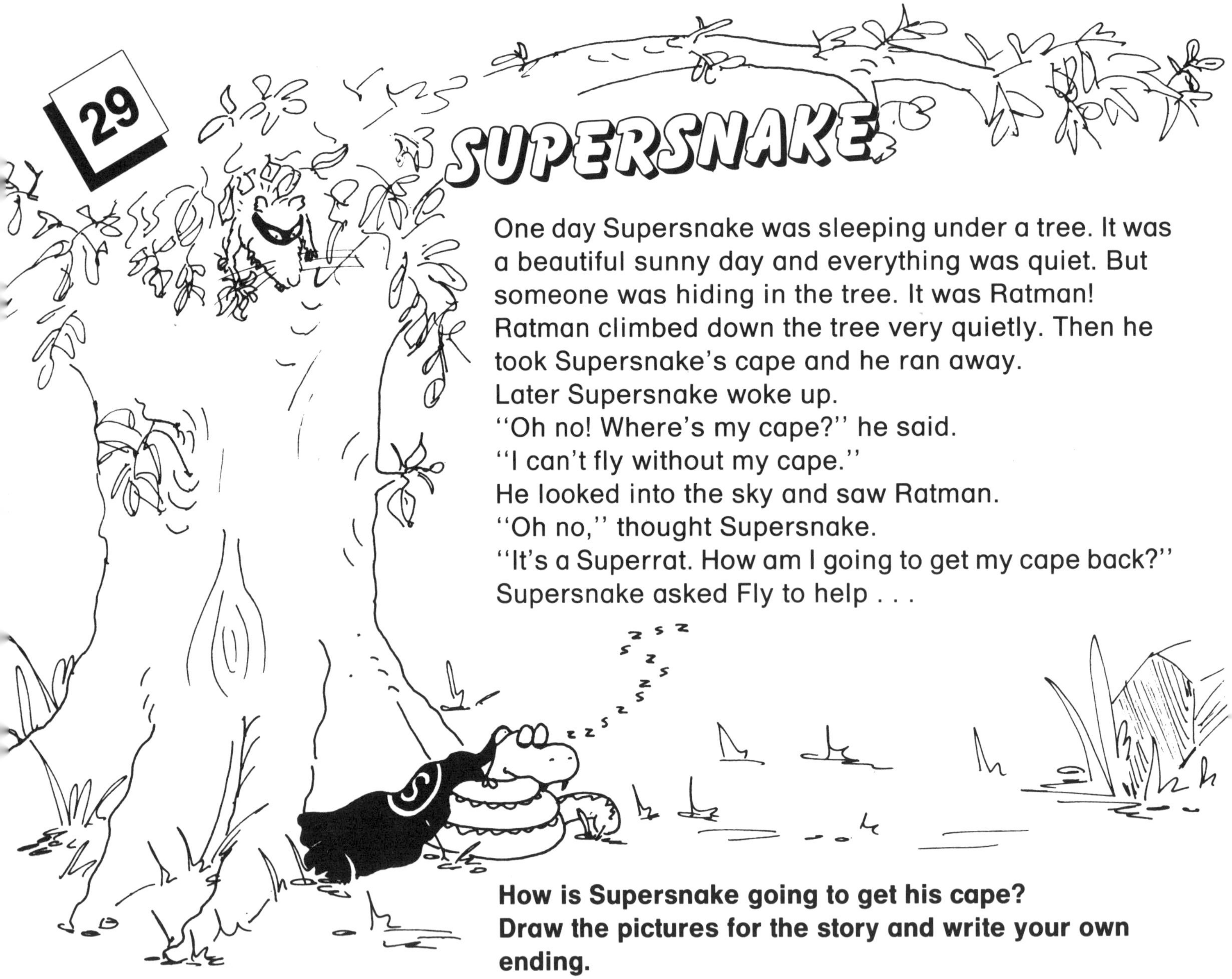

One day Supersnake was sleeping under a tree. It was a beautiful sunny day and everything was quiet. But someone was hiding in the tree. It was Ratman! Ratman climbed down the tree very quietly. Then he took Supersnake's cape and he ran away.

Later Supersnake woke up.

"Oh no! Where's my cape?" he said.

"I can't fly without my cape."

He looked into the sky and saw Ratman.

"Oh no," thought Supersnake.

"It's a Superrat. How am I going to get my cape back?"

Supersnake asked Fly to help . . .

How is Supersnake going to get his cape?
Draw the pictures for the story and write your own ending.

Autobiography

Make your autobiography into a book.

Collect all the pages.
Put all the pages in order.
Write numbers on the pages.

Write a contents page.
Put your book together.

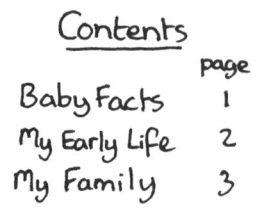

Now find out about a friend. Read their autobiography.

Round-up Unit

r h i n o

r u g

r u l e r a t

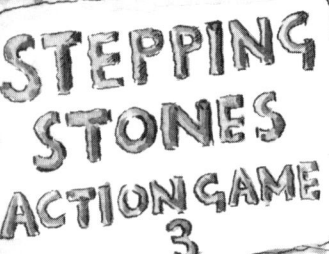

STEPPING STONES ACTION GAME 3

Start here

1. Stand on one leg for 30 seconds.

2. Say a Tongue Twister in English.

3. Whisper the alphabet in English.

4. Write today's date on the blackboard.

5. Walk to the door like a robot.

6. Clap your hands five times.

7. Man-eating prehistoric fish!! Go back five stones.

8. Point to the tallest person in the class.

9. Put your left hand on your head.

10. Touch something rough.

11. Say the months of the year backwards.

12. Tyrannosaurus in the water! Go back eight stones.

13. Don't sit down. Do the opposite.

14. Find a picture of a fish in your Coursebook.

15. Sabre-toothed tiger! Jump forwards to the next stone.

16. Touch the floor near the door.

17. Say 'hello' to the oldest person in the class.

18. Draw a cat on the blackboard without looking.

19. Spell the name of a dinosaur.

20. Whistle an English song.

21. Go and stand behind your teacher.

22. Climb across the dinosaur to stone number twenty-seven.

23. Count backwards in English from twenty to one.

24. Pick up something heavy.

25. Draw a reptile on the blackboard.

26. Touch a girl with the same colour hair as yours.

27. Write the opposite of 'empty'.

28. Say the days of the week backwards.

29. Find someone in your class wearing brown shoes.

30. Touch someone who is taller than you.

31. Write your name without looking.

32. Stamp your feet nine times.

Which book do you need to answer these questions?

1 Do you spell 'addres' like this? ....
2 Where do howler monkeys come from? ....
3 How much did Triceratops weigh? ....
4 How many players are there in a basketball team? ....
5 Where is Luxembourg? ....
6 When was Supersnake born? ....
7 What's on television tonight? ....
8 Are there rings around Neptune? ....

Which one is different? Why?

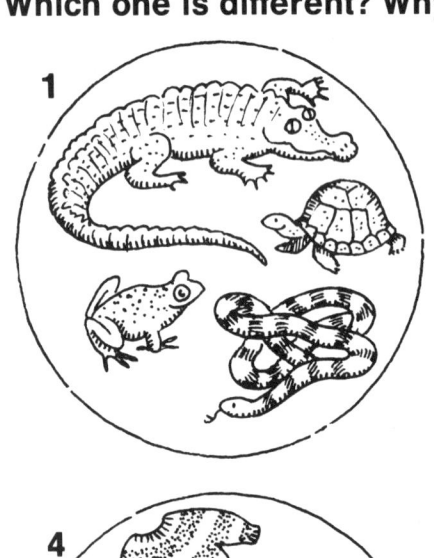

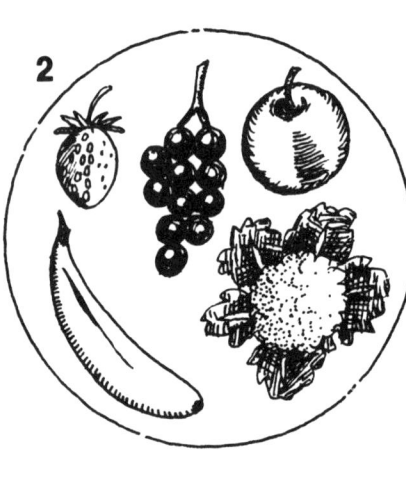

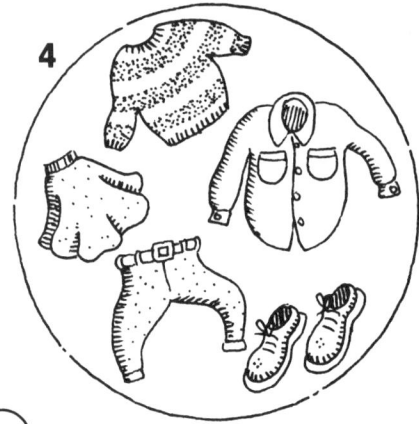

A What is the opposite of these words?

1 started	**3** dark	**5** love	**7** biggest	**9** west	**11** women
2 quickly	**4** smooth	**6** past	**8** older	**10** hot	**12** empty

B Write a word that rhymes with each of these words.

1 why	**3** where	**5** how	**7** which	**9** make	**11** look
2 who	**4** what	**6** when	**8** can	**10** read	**12** true

C These words are all in your Coursebook. What page are they on?

1 deaf	**3** comb	**5** youngest	**7** sharp	**9** mice	**11** digital
2 dirty	**4** lemon	**6** wonderful	**8** seaside	**10** ghost	**12** scissors

D These are small parts of pictures. The pictures are in your Coursebook. What pages are they on?

E Can you read these sentences?

1 This sentence is backwards

2

3

4

Space Passport

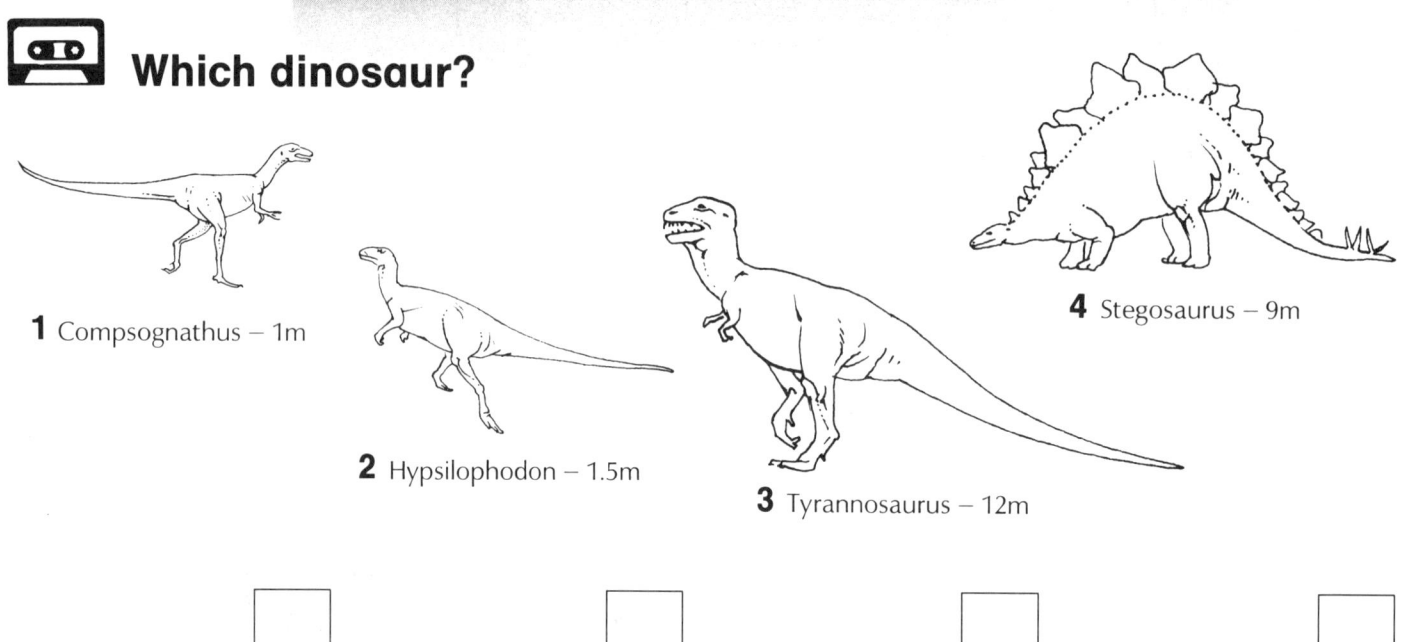

SOLAR SYSTEM PASSPORT

Date of birth ....

Height ....

Weight ....

Hair colour ....

Eye colour ....

VISA JUPITER

PLUTO OCT 2090

Name ....

Address ....

....

....

Nationality ....

Planet ....

Which dinosaur?

1 Compsognathus – 1m

2 Hypsilophodon – 1.5m

3 Tyrannosaurus – 12m

4 Stegosaurus – 9m

Circle the words that you hear on the tape.

cat	bin	pull	hair	bad	sit	ten
cut	bean	pool	here	bath	seat	pen
cup	pin	bull	higher	bat	sight	tent

Use your Reader

A On what page can you find the answer to these questions?

1 Was Pteranodon a dinosaur?
2 What does rain on the glass sound like?
3 What did Arnold see in the park?
4 Who took a photograph of a dinosaur?
5 Who was wearing a new jacket?
6 What kind of animal is a kiwi?
7 How do you get out of Echo Galaxy?
8 Who went to Ancient Egypt in a Time Machine?
9 What is Supersnake eating in the cafe?
10 What planet does Ork-Ork come from?

B Are these sentences true or false?

1 Most of the animals in the world are vertebrates.
2 Archaeopteryx had a long tail.
3 Amphibians lay hard eggs.
4 Hypsilophodon was probably the smallest dinosaur.
5 Most dinosaurs ate plants.
6 Zubians are very clever creatures.
7 The play *Lost in Space* is set in the past.
8 Supersnake wanted to be a fireman.
9 Supersnake's favourite subject at school was maths.
10 Supersnake's friend was called Ratman.

A Look at the pictures on page 61 of your Coursebook.
Write a description of two of the pictures.

B Write 12 sentences. Each sentence must contain one of these words.

1 longest	3 live	5 do	7 can	9 bigger	11 isn't
2 was	4 an	6 have	8 likes	10 are	12 don't

Thomas Nelson and Sons Ltd
Nelson House Mayfield Road
Walton-on-Thames Surrey
KT12 5PL UK

51 York Place
Edinburgh
EH1 3JD UK

Thomas Nelson (Hong Kong) Ltd
Toppan Building 10/F
22a Westlands Road
Quarry Bay Hong Kong

© William Collins Sons & Co Ltd 1990

First published by Collins ELT 1990
ISBN 0-00-370419X

This edition published by Thomas Nelson and Sons Ltd 1993
ISBN 0-17-556669-0
NPN 9 8 7 6 5 4

This Activity Book is accompanied by
Coursebook   ISBN 0-17-556670-4
Teacher's Book ISBN 0-17-556668-2
Cassettes   ISBN 0-17-556633-X

Printed in Hong Kong

Cover artist: David Parkins

Artists: Julie Ashworth, John Batten, Bill Belcher (Anthony
Brandt), Jerry Collins, David Cook (Linden Artists), Peter
Joyce, Dom Mansell, Gillian Martin, David Mostyn, David
Parkins, Jason Pizzey, Pippa Sampson, Nick Schon (Guitty
Talberg), Peter Schrank, Martin Ursell, Louise Voce.

Photos: Ace Photo Agency, Ardea Photographics, J Allan
Cash, Barnaby's Picture Library, Ray Bird, Bruce Coleman
Ltd, Camera Press, John Clark, Mansell Collection, Natural
History Museum, NHPA/Lacz Lemoine, NHPA/Mandal
Ranjit, NHPA/Jany Sauvanet, Robert Harding Picture
Library, Chris Ridgers, Toyota, WWF UK/Paul Coppi, WWF
UK/M White, Zefa, Zoo Operations Ltd. Photographs on
pages 17, 33, 35, 39 and 45 by Trevor Clifford, with art
direction by Sandie Huskinson-Rolfe (Photoseekers).
R2-D2 courtesy of Lucasfilm Ltd

The publishers would also like to thank The Royal
Association in aid of Deaf People for permission to
reproduce the sign language alphabet on page 39 and The
Colour Museum, Bradford for their research on optical
illusions (page 37)

Typesetting by Chambers Wallace